I0797379

THE MAYA MYTHS

THE MAYA MYTHS

A GUIDE TO THE GODS, HEROES AND ANCESTORS

MALLORY E. MATSUMOTO

Dedicated to Maya storytellers past, present, and future.

HALF-TITLE A mosaic ornament depicting a monkey scribe, originally part of a pair, from El Peru-Waka', Petén, Guatemala, mid-seventh century CE.

FRONTISPIECE Relief of Muwaan Bahlam as a captive impersonating jaguar deity, from Tonina, Chiapas, Mexico, *c.* 700 CE.

First published in the United Kingdom in 2025 by
Thames & Hudson Ltd, 6–24 Britannia Street, London WC1X 9JD

First published in the United States of America in 2025 by
Thames & Hudson Inc., 500 Fifth Avenue, New York, New York 10110

EU Authorized Representative: Interart S.A.R.L.
19 rue Charles Auray, 93500 Pantin, Paris, France
productsafety@thameshudson.co.uk
interart.fr

A CIP catalogue record for this book is available from the British Library

Library of Congress Control Number 2024947073

ISBN 978-0-500-02654-0
01

Printed and bound in China by Toppan Leefung Printing Limited

CONTENTS

The Maya Region

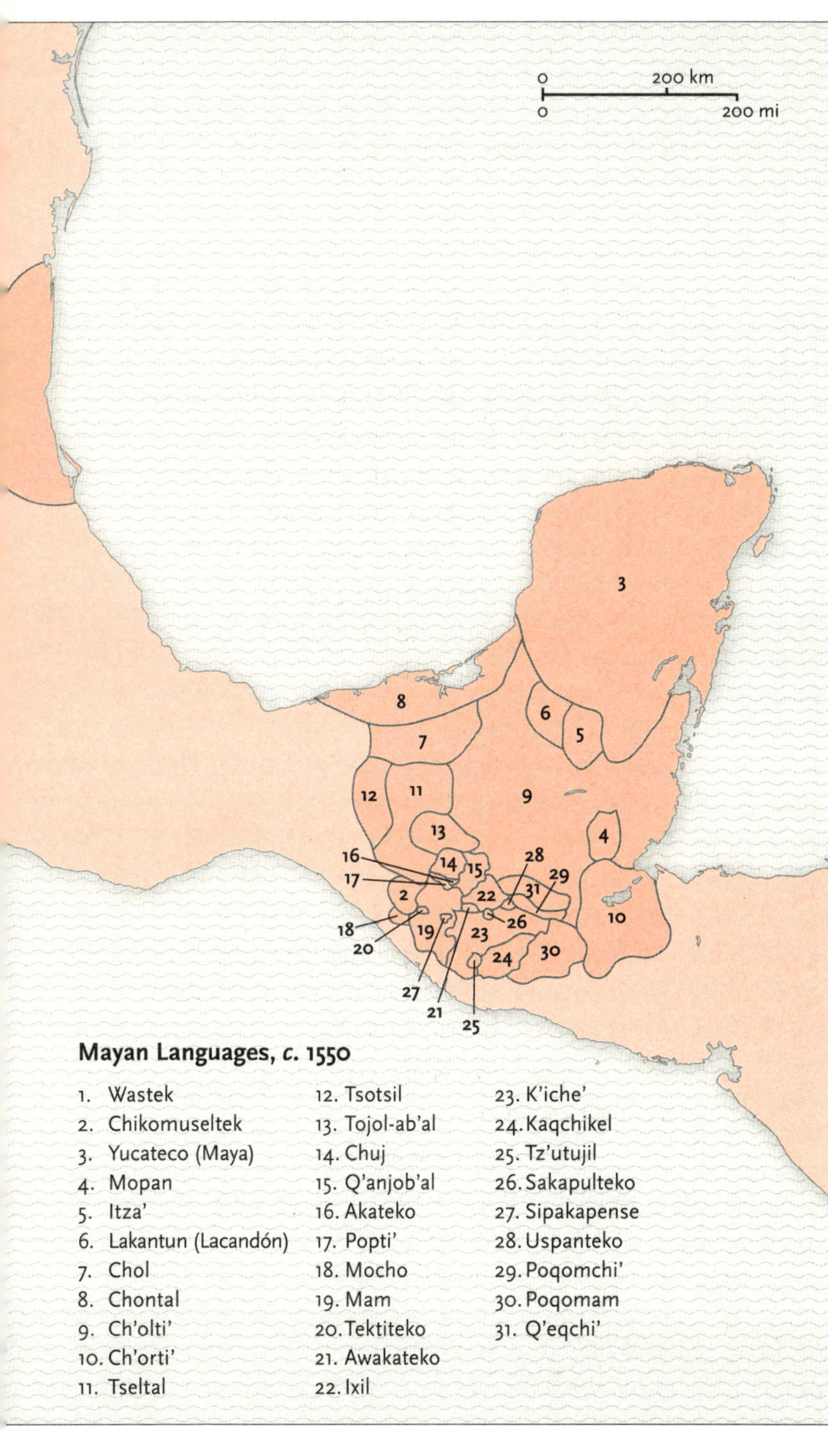
0
200 km
0
200 mi
1
2
3
4
5
6
7
8
9
10
11
12
13
14
15
16
17
18
19
20
21
22
23
24
25
26
27
28
29
30
31
Mayan Languages, *c.* 1550
1. Wastek
2. Chikomuseltek
3. Yucateco (Maya)
4. Mopan
5. Itza'
6. Lakantun (Lacandón)
7. Chol
8. Chontal
9. Ch'olti'
10. Ch'orti'
11. Tseltal
12. Tsotsil
13. Tojol-ab'al
14. Chuj
15. Q'anjob'al
16. Akateko
17. Popti'
18. Mocho
19. Mam
20. Tektiteko
21. Awakateko
22. Ixil
23. K'iche'
24. Kaqchikel
25. Tz'utujil
26. Sakapulteko
27. Sipakapense
28. Uspanteko
29. Poqomchi'
30. Poqomam
31. Q'eqchi'

INTRODUCTION

> This is the account of when all is still silent and placid. All is silent and calm. Hushed and empty is the womb of the sky. These, then, are the first words, the first speech. There is not yet one person, one animal, bird, fish, crab, tree, rock, hollow, canyon, meadow, or forest. All alone the sky exists. The face of the earth has not yet appeared. Alone lies the expanse of the sea, along with the womb of all the sky. There is not yet anything gathered together. All is at rest. Nothing stirs. All is languid, at rest in the sky. There is not yet anything standing erect. Only the expanse of the water, only the tranquil sea lies alone. There is not yet anything that might exist. All lies placid and silent in the darkness, in the night.
>
> *Popol Vuh*, mid-sixteenth century, translation by Allen Christenson (2007: 67–68)

According to the K'iche' Maya *Popol Vuh*, the primordial world was dark. The sea was calm, the sky dim, the air quiet. Nothing moved. There were no animals, no plants. People did not yet walk the earth. But there were words—words that, once spoken, brought the first creation to light and to life.

The myths of the Maya are as old as the Maya themselves. They are also as dynamic as the people who tell them. After their creation, the Maya were by all accounts an undifferentiated mass, lacking the ethnic and cultural identities that have distinguished them for as long as we can trace back their histories. Gradually, they split into dozens of ethnolinguistic groups and spread across the lowlands and highlands of southern Mesoamerica. In the process, they developed distinct identities rooted in the places where they lived, the objects that they made, the food that they ate, and the words that they spoke. At the same time, they continuously interacted with other Maya and non-Maya groups around them. The stories that Maya peoples tell about themselves and their world reflect this deep history. The same history is refracted in the stories that archaeologists, historians, anthropologists, and other academics tell about the Maya.

Timeline

Early Preclassic: 2000–1000 BCE
Middle Preclassic: 1000–350 BCE
Late Preclassic: 350–50 BCE
Terminal Preclassic: 50 BCE–250 CE
Early Classic: 250–600
Late Classic: 600–820
Terminal Classic: 820–925
Early Postclassic: 925–1200
Late Postclassic: 1200–1524
Colonial: 1524–1821
Republican: 1821–present

MAYA HISTORIES: A BRIEF OVERVIEW

The Maya region is divided into two major geographic areas: the lowlands to the north and east, and the highlands to the south and west. As the name suggests, the lowlands are largely flat, and the highest elevations generally reach no more than 390 m (1,280 ft) above sea level. The climate is subtropical, with thick vegetation ranging in character from dry forest and scrublands in the northern Yucatán peninsula to tropical moist forests to the south. Natural surface water is limited across this karst landscape, especially in the north. Precipitation seeps through porous limestone bedrock into the underground aquifer, which is accessible through caves and sinkholes, or *cenotes* (from Yucatec *ts'onóot*).

The highlands, in turn, consist of a stretch of mountainous terrain concentrated in what are now Chiapas, Mexico, and the western half of Guatemala. Elevation ranges from 1,000 m to over 4,000 m (3,280–13,120 ft) above sea level. Even today, steep valleys and canyons make travel laborious and time-consuming between points that are close as the crow flies. The temperate climate is relatively mild, although temperatures can drop below freezing in winter in higher-altitude areas, especially in western Guatemala. The environment varies according to precipitation level and altitude, from montane humid forests up to grasslands and shrublands at higher elevations. The highlands are also home to the region's major volcanoes, of which several remain active.

Across the Maya region, alternating rainy and dry seasons define the annual cycle, although the yearly total rainfall varies dramatically between the relatively arid northern lowlands and the much wetter western and southern lowlands. The cycle between wet and dry seasons has defined the millennia-long tradition of *milpa*, an agricultural system of intercropping centered on maize. Historically, rainfall was concentrated during the months of May to October; conversely, precipitation was minimal during the warmer, dry season from November to April. Today, though, climate change is causing local weather patterns to shift in unfamiliar, often unpredictable ways.

A limestone lintel looted from the Classic Maya site of Laxtunich depicts king Shield Jaguar IV of Yaxchilan, Chiapas, Mexico (top left), receiving from his vassal Aj Chak Maax (right) a trio of captives (bottom left). According to the hieroglyphic text between the king and his subordinate, the presentation occurred on August 23, 783, three days after the captives had been seized.

The earliest archaeological evidence for human occupation in the Maya area dates to approximately 13,000 years ago during the Late Pleistocene, a period of climatic fluctuation and major megafauna extinction. The nomadic hunter-gatherers gradually adopted pottery, a sedentary lifestyle, and agriculture, including domesticated maize, over the course of some 10,000 years. For unknown reasons, these transformations took almost a millennium longer in the Maya area compared to elsewhere in Mesoamerica.

By the Middle Preclassic period, archaeologists can identify the first expressions of cultural features that they classify as "Maya," including aggregated settlements with monumental architecture, ballcourts, ritual deposits or caches, and coherent ceramic traditions. The Late Preclassic and Terminal Preclassic periods are characterized by the oldest excavated evidence of hieroglyphic writing. The earliest texts include evidence of the complex calendrical system that the Maya would continue to develop over the next two-and-a-half millennia, into the present day.

The Classic period saw significant population growth, settlement expansion, and general cultural fluorescence in the lowlands. Divine, dynastic kings—and, occasionally, queens—ruled over dozens of discrete but interconnected polities, their authority deriving from their capacity to mediate relations with the gods and ancestors by performing rituals on behalf of the larger community. Conflict over resources was common, and some polities achieved regional prowess through a combination of military success and alliance-building. The Kaanul dynasty at Dzibanche and Calakmul and the Mutul dynasty at Tikal consolidated control across swaths of the central lowlands in alternating cycles of ascent and decline that often lasted no more than a generation or two. Not even these hegemons ever achieved anything close to political unification of the Maya region, however.

The Classic period is the best-understood span of Maya history prior to European contact due to a relative abundance of hieroglyphic records. The 12,000 known Maya texts represent a period of nearly two millennia, between 300 BCE and 1500 CE, but most were written during the Late Classic period, when population and settlement density peaked. Many Mesoamerican groups, from the Olmecs on Mexico's Gulf Coast to the Aztecs in central Mexico, developed forms of writing. However, the Maya are the only civilization in the Indigenous Americas to create a robust script that, much like the alphabet in which this book is written, could accurately and comprehensively record spoken language. The Maya script consisted of two basic kinds of hieroglyphs: logographs, each representing a word or idea; and syllabic signs, each denoting a consonant–vowel sequence

A polychrome ceramic vase excavated from a young woman's tomb at Tikal, Petén, Guatemala, shows local king Yax Nuun Ahiin II (center right) as a warrior facing his richly attired queen (center left). The royal couple is flanked by two attendants in a courtly scene that the hieroglyphic text between them dates to June 11, 794.

with no associated meaning. Of some 1,000 distinct hieroglyphs in the writing system, about one-third remain to be deciphered.

Following the collapse of divine kingship and the existing social order at the end of the Classic period, most major settlements in the central and southern lowlands were abandoned. The epicenter of Postclassic Maya civilization shifted to the northern lowlands of the Yucatán peninsula and the highlands of what are now Chiapas and Guatemala. In the former area, Chichen Itza and later Mayapan

---

Tula and the Toltecs

One of the longest-raging controversies in Maya archaeology revolves around the Toltec empire and its influence on Maya civilization. Archaeologists generally consider the best candidate for the Toltec capital to be the site of Tula in Hidalgo, Mexico, just over 70 km (40 miles) north of modern-day Mexico City. Retroactive histories contend that the Toltecs arrived there in the Late Classic period after several generations of migration. By the Terminal Classic period, the Toltec empire's cultural and political reach extended into the northern Maya lowlands. Its influence among the Maya manifested in the construction of Toltec-style architecture, integration of Toltec motifs into local iconography, and adoption of the cult of the feathered serpent (see Chapter 6), among other phenomena. Since the mid-nineteenth century, scholars have disputed the forces underlying the cultural shift toward Toltec influence among the Postclassic Maya. Was there a military invasion? Amplified trade contacts? Mass Toltec migration to the Yucatán peninsula? The historical context remains murky, but it is clear that there was intensive contact and interpersonal exchange between the two regions and that Toltec culture exercised significant influence on Terminal Classic and Early Postclassic Maya civilization.

---

stood out as major urban centers where political and economic power concentrated. Influence from central Mexico and especially from the Toltecs is most apparent at Chichen Itza, where similarities in architecture, iconography, and material culture indicate direct, intensive exchange. Mayapan, which was governed by a council of confederated lineages or houses rather than a dynasty of divine kings, maintained extensive trade networks with the central Maya lowlands, as well as with non-Maya peoples in the Caribbean, the Gulf Coast, and central Mexico. The Postclassic lowlands were the last bastion of Maya hieroglyphic writing, too, where it remained in active use through the sixteenth century.

In the highlands, the primary power broker during the Postclassic period was the K'iche' confederation. Its capital, Q'umarkaaj, was founded around the turn of the fifteenth century and flourished until conquistador Pedro de Alvarado and his invading army razed it in 1524. K'iche' preeminence did not go uncontested, however. In 1470, one group within the confederation, the Kaqchikel, rebelled and founded their own polity based at Chi Iximche'. Another polity, the Tz'utujil, controlled trade routes between the temperate highlands and the steamy Pacific coast with its lucrative cacao orchards from its capital at the Chi Ya' on the shores of Lake Atitlán. All three highland groups were integrated into exchange networks that reached as far north as central Mexico. By the sixteenth century, the K'iche' and Kaqchikel were even paying tribute to the Aztec emperor in distant Tenochtitlan (now Mexico City).

The first Spanish expedition to the Yucatán peninsula landed in 1517. The next year, Juan de Grijalva returned to the Yucatán in search of gold. Hernán Cortés's fleet also landed on the peninsula in 1519 on its way to the Gulf Coast, in the expedition that would ultimately result in the conquest of Tenochtitlan in 1521. Early European–Maya encounters resulted in some skirmishes, but did not prompt concerted Spanish effort to gain military control or establish settlements. Instead, Guatemala would be the target of the first Spanish-led invasion of the Maya region.

The K'iche' and Kaqchikel heard about the foreign invaders' takeover of Tenochtitlan through their central Mexican contacts and sent emissaries to Cortés and his conquistadors in 1522. Following Mesoamerican custom, the joint mission brought gifts to Cortés as tribute, intended to preempt a military invasion. Unfamiliar with Indigenous diplomacy, the Spaniards saw the gesture as an enticing preview of the visitors' material wealth. Encouraged by the promise of riches to the south, Cortés sent Alvarado and a small army to continue the conquest down the Pacific coast in late 1523.

Bolstered by several thousand Indigenous allies recruited along the way, Alvarado's army achieved initial battlefield successes against

This scene painted on a ceramic vase shows a Classic Maya king receiving seven cloaked visitors and their gifts, which are being presented to the king by courtiers. The vessel was deposited in the tomb of king Jasaw Chan K'awiil I of Tikal in the first half of the eighth century CE.

the K'iche' in early 1524. The victories prompted the Kaqchikel to ally with the Spaniards in April 1524, initially to subdue the rival Tz'utujil polity at Chi Ya'. By August of that year, however, the alliance collapsed after the Kaqchikel rebelled against Alvarado's burdensome tribute demands. The conquistador briefly left the Maya region to continue pushing southward to conquer Nawat (Pipil), Xinka, and other non-Maya peoples farther down the Pacific coast. After a series of losses, Alvarado returned to Guatemala with his army in late 1525 to consolidate control of the western highlands. By 1530, the Kaqchikel were forced to surrender, marking the capitulation of the last major Maya polity in the area.

While Alvarado was engaged in Guatemala, Cortés led his own expedition with thousands of Mexican warriors to Honduras. They traversed a large swath of the lowlands, from Tabasco into the central Petén, where they made first European contact with the Itza' Maya at Nojpeten (Tayasal) on the shores of Lake Petén Itzá. Concerted efforts to conquer the Maya lowlands did not begin until several years later, however, when Francisco de Montejo, who had accompanied Cortés to Honduras, led a return expedition to the Yucatán in late 1527. By 1546, the Spanish had secured control over the northern Yucatán peninsula, but their jurisdiction over the southern peninsula remained nominal until 1697, when the Itza', the last independent Maya kingdom, fell. For the remainder of the colonial period, Spanish settlement and administrative reach remained strongest in the areas of early conquest in the western highlands and northern lowlands and considerably weaker in the central, western, and southern lowlands and eastern highlands.

Today, the Maya region stretches across five nation-states. Mexico, Guatemala, Honduras, and El Salvador achieved independence from Spain in 1821, whereas Belize remained a British colony until 1981. Of these countries, Guatemala is home to the largest Maya population, in terms of both absolute number and proportion of total population. The 2018 census counted over 7 million Maya persons, representing more than 40 percent of Guatemalans, but the number is considered an underestimate. Maya ethnic identity is intimately associated with Mayan language skills and traditional dress and is still widely stigmatized. As a result, many Maya persons—especially men, who are much less likely than women to regularly wear traditional clothing or speak a Mayan language—self-identify as non-Indigenous.

In all five countries, Maya peoples are overrepresented among statistics of poverty and violence, a consequence of systemic oppression and deprivation dating back to the colonial period. In the worst cases, prejudice has taken violent expression. Between 1960 and 1996, up to 200,000 persons were murdered or disappeared in Guatemala's genocidal civil war. More than 80 percent of these victims were Maya. Although leftist guerrillas also terrorized the civilian population, a later investigation sponsored by the United Nations concluded that the Guatemalan military and its paramilitary affiliates—whose financial and logistical backers included the United States—had been responsible for more than 90 percent of the killings and disappearances.

The late twentieth century also saw the birth of the Pan-Maya movement in Guatemala to advocate for Maya peoples' political and cultural rights. Although the movement's success has been mixed, Maya persons are slowly gaining representation in regional and national politics. The highest-profile case to date has been Mam activist and politician Thelma Cabrera Pérez de Sánchez, who won an unprecedented 10.3 percent of the popular vote in the 2018 presidential election. She was considered enough of a political threat that Guatemala's electoral court denied her candidacy in the 2023 election, in a decision that observers widely criticized as partisan and undemocratic. Other gains include legislation mandating access to bilingual education and government services in Indigenous languages. Since 1990, the Guatemalan Academy of Mayan Languages (Academia de Lenguas Mayas) has been tasked with protecting and promoting the country's twenty-two Mayan languages. Mayan languages spoken in Mexico are supported by the cognate National Indigenous Languages Institute (Instituto Nacional de Lenguas Indígenas). Nonetheless, legal protections of Indigenous rights remain much stronger on paper than in practice. Racial, cultural, and linguistic discrimination against Indigenous peoples are still widespread barriers to social advancement in all five countries in the Maya region.

WHO ARE THE MAYA?

Today, the term "Maya" is used to indicate diverse communities with a common ethnolinguistic background. This usage is relatively new, however. "Maya" was first used in this capacity in the Yucatán peninsula, where its most common usage was in the name with which speakers of Yucatec Maya still refer to their language, *maya' t'àan*. Prior to the mid-eighteenth century, the word was rarely used to refer to people. When it was, it usually indicated persons outside of one's own community who were considered inferior in some way. Only after the civil or "caste" war in the Yucatán in the

1840s and 1850s and the rise of archaeology in the region in the late nineteenth century did the term "Maya" take on wider currency as an ethnonym.

Until the late twentieth century, "Maya" was almost exclusively used as an exonym. In other words, it was applied by outsiders to a diverse collection of peoples who did not self-identify as part of a larger group. Since the 1980s, however, Pan-Maya leaders have promoted a unified Maya identity as a vehicle for political solidarity. Bolstered by government-supported marketing for heritage tourism, the movement has prompted more Indigenous individuals to embrace a regional Maya identity in addition to traditional, local forms of self-affiliation. Nonetheless, those who self-identify as "Maya" still represent a minority of the people to whom scholars and bureaucrats would apply that ethnolinguistic label.

The Maya region's geographic contours have remained essentially the same for more than three millennia. But it has never had clear political boundaries of the sort that we like to draw on our maps today. Unlike, say, imperial China or pharaonic Egypt, the Maya region has never been unified. Despite some popularized claims to the contrary, there has never been a Maya empire or regional state. Traditionally, Maya identity has been closely tied to lineage and village. As far as linguists and historians can tell, there was no term by which the ancient inhabitants of the Maya region referred collectively to themselves. For all their political differences, however, the Classic Maya did recognize themselves as belonging to the same civilization. They portrayed each other with a wide but consistent range of physical features—including teardrop-shaped eyes, minimal facial hair, robust lips,

Classic Maya musicians beat drums and shake rattles while parading in distinctive white, feathered headdresses in a late eighth-century mural from Bonampak, Chiapas, Mexico.

and an elongated cranium—and sporting familiar accessories like earspools, beaded necklaces, and hipcloths (for men) or dress-like *huipiles* (for women). Non-Maya peoples like the Toltecs or the inhabitants of Teotihuacan were represented in contrasting poses, with faces, dress, and accoutrements marking them as distinctly "other." Ancient Maya communities did not share a regional identity based on social or political ties, yet they perceived a basic cultural affiliation that distinguished them from foreign, non-Maya peoples.

Teotihuacan

Of all Mesoamerican civilizations with which the ancient Maya engaged, Teotihuacan (pronounced *Tay-oh-tee-WA-kan*) seems to have loomed largest in their collective imagination. Teotihuacan was probably settled around the first century BCE; by the Early Classic period, the cosmopolitan metropolis dominated life in the Valley of Mexico and beyond. What was at the time the largest city in the Americas engaged in pan-Mesoamerican trade networks and housed a multiethnic population that included enclaves of Maya, Zapotec, and other Mesoamerican migrants. The ethnolinguistic identity of Teotihuacan's inhabitants is a source of controversy, and its pictorial writing system remains undeciphered. Their cultural and political influence during the Early Classic period, however, is undeniable.

Archaeologists have traced evidence of Teotihuacan's cultural influence as far south as Maya settlements at Copan and along Guatemala's Pacific coast. The Early Classic founder of Copan's ruling dynasty is said to have traveled all the way to the distant polity to be confirmed in his authority as king back home. Material culture associated with the central Mexican polity, including intricately modeled incense burners, an architectural feature known

WHAT IS A MYTH?

In keeping with the other books in this series, the narratives presented here are called "myths." The term's use requires important qualifications. According to popular use of the English word today, a "myth" is an account that lacks historical accuracy or cannot be proven to be true—and can thus be dismissed as false by others. Yet a myth's social and cultural power does not depend on the truth value of its contents. Instead, a myth's salience is based on its capacity to clarify

as *talud-tablero*, and tripod ceramic vessels, is widespread across the Maya region from the Early Classic period. Teotihuacan is also the only Mesoamerican civilization whose representatives are known to have intervened directly in Classic Maya politics. According to hieroglyphic records, an entourage of Teotihuacanos dethroned and executed the king of Tikal, Chak Tok Ich'aak I, in 378 and installed a new dynastic line in his place.

Teotihuacan declined and was abandoned rather abruptly in the mid-sixth century for reasons that remain unclear. The polity's legacy long survived its capital, however. Into the Terminal Classic period, lowland Maya kings continued to portray themselves as cultural and political inheritors of the central Mexican civilization. The Aztecs, who founded their imperial capital of Tenochtitlan just to the south of the long-abandoned city, considered it to be "the place of the gods"—*Teōtīhuacān* in their language, Nahuatl—and made recurrent pilgrimages there, even excavating ancient artifacts to deposit as offerings in Tenochtitlan's ceremonial precinct. Even now, as Mexico City's urban sprawl gradually envelops it, Teotihuacan is one of Mexico's most-visited archaeological sites, second only to the Maya city of Chichen Itza.

some aspect of the teller's reality. Understanding "myths" as stories that explain, contextualize, or justify more closely approximates to how the Maya thought and continue to think about the tales presented here.

There is no native Maya equivalent for the Western concept of "myth." Colonial-period Maya renderings of what the Spanish called *mitos* tended to emphasize the tales' historical purview rather than any religious connotations they might have. The Maya stories about the past recounted in this book, like so many others that the following pages could not accommodate, are more accurately understood as "mythohistory." Anthropologist Frank Salomon coined this neologism to capture the inseparability in Indigenous American traditions of what the Western world considers two distinct narrative genres, myth and history. Whether or not the accounts represent events or actors that "really happened" or existed in an empirical sense is not the point, neither for authors nor for audiences. What matters most is how the narratives account for their communities' present realities and future prospects.

Unlike the Catholic religion that the Spaniards introduced to the region in the sixteenth century, Maya religion(s) have never had sacred texts or scriptures that were widely accepted or consulted. The *Popol Vuh* is sometimes referred to popularly as a "Maya Bible." That moniker is inaccurate and misleading. The text was composed for a local audience and was not widely circulated. Moreover, its K'iche' Maya authors did not assume the contents, ranging from mythology and cosmology to history and genealogy, to be uniquely definitive or credible. They expressed a worldview that was fundamental to their community's identity, knowing full well that it existed alongside other, competing worldviews around them.

For these reasons, it would not be possible to assemble a compendium of the greatest Maya mythological hits or to compile a roster of the most important gods. To claim otherwise would give this book a historical authority that it does not deserve. Each narrative was chosen because it touches upon a larger theme relevant to understanding Maya civilization. To the greatest extent possible in such a modest forum, they make a collective effort to represent the breadth of diversity encompassed under the simplifying umbrella of "Maya." All share a retrospective perspective, narrating events that happened in the ancestral or even primordial past, before the narrators' own lifetimes. Their authors are Maya persons who were recounting, sometimes collaboratively, stories that circulated in oral tradition before they were written down in hieroglyphs or the Roman alphabet. Most of the storytellers' names are unknown to us today. But their compositions reflect a unique perspective on the past and that past's relevance to the present and future.

THE MAYA MYTHS

The six chapters of this book each recount two to four myths that share a common theme. Chapter 1 addresses the beginning of the Maya cosmos, including its quadripartite structure and multiple creations. Chapter 2 accounts for the origins of the sun and the moon, which assumed their places in the sky after a series of primordial confrontations that pre-date the dawn of the first humans. The stories in Chapter 3 consider the relationship between the celestial realm and the underworld, the abode of the gods and ancestors whose affairs continue to shape life on the earth in between.

Since its ancient origins, maize has been the foundation of traditional Maya subsistence. Chapter 4 highlights this essential foodstuff with the biography of the Classic Maya Maize god, an account of how the ancestors first acquired maize as a crop, and a myth about the reciprocal relations that define milpa agriculture into the present. Chapter 5 explores the origins of Maya peoples and the primordial contexts in which they differentiated into distinct ethnolinguistic groups. Finally, Chapter 6 presents two myths about apical ancestors whose arrival from a far-off land marked a sea change in the identity and history of the local Maya community.

Pronunciation Guide

Today, Mayan languages are written in a modified Roman alphabet that Spanish missionaries first introduced during the colonial period. Orthographic conventions vary between languages and region, so readers may notice slight variations. In very general terms, vowels and many consonants are pronounced more or less as they are in English or Spanish. The sounds most different from European languages are glottal stop and a series of glottalized or ejective consonants, all marked by an apostrophe (') and pronounced by briefly constricting outward airflow through the glottis. They are among a modest number of letter-sound combinations that may be unfamiliar to English or Spanish speakers:

Letter	International Phonetic Alphabet Symbol	English Comparison
b'	ɓ	similar to ***ball***, but with minimal release of air on the first consonant
ch'	ʧ'	like *ca**tch***, with a more forceful push of air behind the final consonant
j	χ	similar to *lo**ch***, but with the back of the tongue raised toward the uvula
k'	k'	like *pe**ck***, with a more forceful push of air behind the final consonant
q	q	similar to ***k**ale*, but with the back of the tongue raised toward the uvula
q'	q'	(glottalized q)
t'	t'	like *ca**t***, with a more forceful push of air behind the final consonant
tz	ts	*bee**ts***
tz'	ts'	like *bee**ts***, with a more forceful push of air behind the final syllable
x	ʃ	***sh**ip*
'	ʔ	the brief catch of air between syllables in *uh-oh*

Sources for the myths date to anywhere from the eighth to the early twenty-first century. Their geographic origins span the lowlands of the Yucatán in the northeast through the Guatemalan highlands to the southwest. Some stories have been translated from hieroglyphic inscriptions or reconstructed from ancient imagery; others have come down to us in alphabetic texts transcribed during the colonial period or recorded by modern ethnographers. Some are drawn from relatively well-known Maya sources like the *Popol Vuh* or the *Books of Chilam Balam* from the Yucatán peninsula. Others are less familiar, and even specialists likely will encounter one or two tales with which they are not acquainted.

Individually, each myth represents a slice of one person's or group's conception of the Maya cosmos. Collectively, they provide a glimpse of the richness of histories that have been shaped by generations of change and exchange with other Mesoamericans and, since the sixteenth century, with Europeans, Africans, and Asians. They are histories that Maya communities continue to write today.

1

CREATIONS

There is no shared, canonical Maya narrative of the creation of the cosmos or its earliest inhabitants. The many variations apparent in surviving creation stories suggest that such a singular account probably never existed. Each of the dozens, if not hundreds, of creation stories recorded since pre-colonial times reflects a combination of widespread beliefs about the state of humanity and its universe and the preoccupations and experiences of the local community in which the story was told.

Basic contours of a Maya cosmogony, or account of the origins of the cosmos, appear when comparing stories about the primordial past. One consistent trope is that the cosmos was not a primordial given but was created in stages by a small cohort of divine beings. The Maya cosmos is neither the product of a single creation episode, nor is it static. A diverse series of actors has shaped and reshaped its manifold features numerous times since creation. Even today, the cosmos is being influenced by its current inhabitants—us.

THE CREATION OF THE *WINALS*

The creation of time coincided with the primordial forging of the Maya cosmos. This event is recorded in the so-called *Books of Chilam Balam* penned in Chumayel, Yucatán, by Yucatec Maya scribe Juan

José Hoil during the late eighteenth century. The story chronicles the creation of the first *winal*, a twenty-day period in the traditional Maya calendar. It also accounts for the origins of the 260-day ritual calendar, whose four-part structure correlates to the basic layout of the cosmos. Composed in the Yucatec language, it is likely that a sage or priest originally sang the text before it was first written down in alphabetic script during the colonial period.

Classic Maya calendar glyphs from Quirigua, Izabal, Guatemala, 766 CE.

The 260-Day Ritual Calendar

The ancient Maya developed a highly sophisticated calendrical system that could precisely track time and accurately predict astronomical phenomena like solar and lunar eclipses. Of over a dozen known calendrical cycles, the most widespread and enduring has been the 260-day ritual calendar, which the Maya inherited from and shared with other Mesoamerican peoples. It has traditionally been the primary calendar among ritual specialists for divination and is maintained in some highland Maya communities to this day.

The 260-day calendar consists of twenty named days and thirteen numerical prefixes. The first day in the Classic Maya version was 1 Imix, followed by 2 Ik', 3 Ak'bal, 4 K'an, and so forth. After the thirteenth day, 13 Ben, the numerical prefixes reset while the day names continued down the list. The count continued with 1 Ix as day fourteen, 2 Men as day fifteen, until reaching the twentieth and final named day, 7 Ajaw. Thereafter, the list of day names reset while the numerical prefixes continued, making the twenty-first day 8 Imix, the twenty-second day 9 Ik', and so on. After 260 days, the cycle reached the day 1 Imix and began the count anew.

The story goes that the first wiseman, Melchisedek, and diviner, Na Puc Tun, sang to us of a time in the deep past, before our world was created, before the first winal. It was then that four women set off in search of a god. As the women—the god's maternal grandmother, aunt, paternal grandmother, and sister-in-law—walked down the road, they asked themselves, "What shall we say when we shall see a human being on a road?" But there were, in fact, no humans, for humans had not yet been created.

The four women converged in the east, where they saw a series of footprints on the ground. They determined that the tracks belonged to the god whom they sought, and one of the group, a goddess named U Colel Cab ("Wife of the World"), placed her foot in the print. With her own foot atop the trace of his, U Colel Cab measured the footprint of the great god, our Father (*Dios citbil*), and said that this mark was the beginning of the count of the world. Twelve more imprints stretched before them, leading to 13 Ok, the thirteenth mark. At the end of the line, 13 Ok was the birthplace and time of the great god.

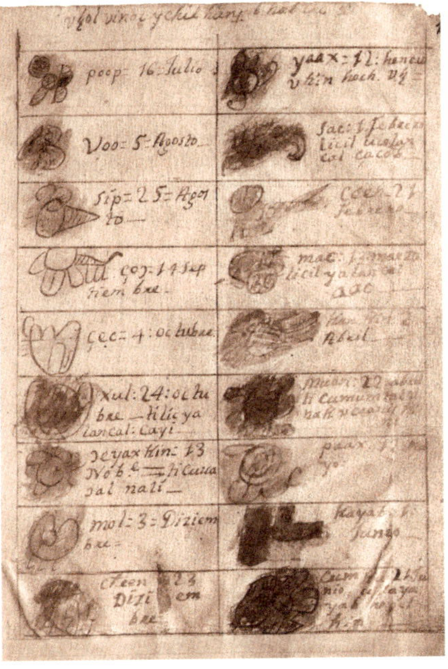

A table from the *Chilam Balam of Chumayel* (fol. 13r) recording the eighteen months of the 365-day solar calendar. Alongside alphabetic text in each quadrant are signs that may well represent the latest known attempt to write Maya hieroglyphs. The signs are so abstracted, however, that they were clearly copied by someone who could no longer read the by-then abandoned script.

The *Books of Chilam Balam*

Juan José Hoil's handwritten manuscript from Chumayel is one of several known today as the *Books of Chilam Balam*. The manuscripts are named after a Postclassic oracle (Yucatec *chilan* or *chilam*) named Balam ("Jaguar"), who was believed to have prophesied the coming of the first Europeans and the Spanish conquest of the Yucatán. Each *Chilam Balam* manuscript or "book" is a compilation of diverse contents, many of which were probably copied from earlier texts, including ones first written in the Maya hieroglyphic script. They cover topics ranging from creation mythology and agricultural almanacs to European astrology, histories of the Spanish conquest, and prophecies about the future, making them invaluable sources about Postclassic and colonial-period Yucatec culture and society.

The god and his maternal grandmother, aunt, paternal grandmother, and sister-in-law retraced the god's steps to where he had been born in the east, where it had all begun. When they reached 13 Ok in the east, U Colel Cab spoke the god's name. At that time, the day still did not have a name. When U Colel Cab spoke, the winal was born there in the east. The name of the day was born. Thus began the means by which the sky and the earth were born; the water descended to the earth; and the stones, the trees, and the creatures of the sea and of the land were born.

Following the footsteps, the five divine beings let the cosmos take shape. It was formed in a series of events, of which each was associated with one day in the first winal. The first day of this first winal, 1 Chuwen, was the day when the earth and the sky were shaped. On the next day, 2 Eb, the first stairway was fashioned. It came down

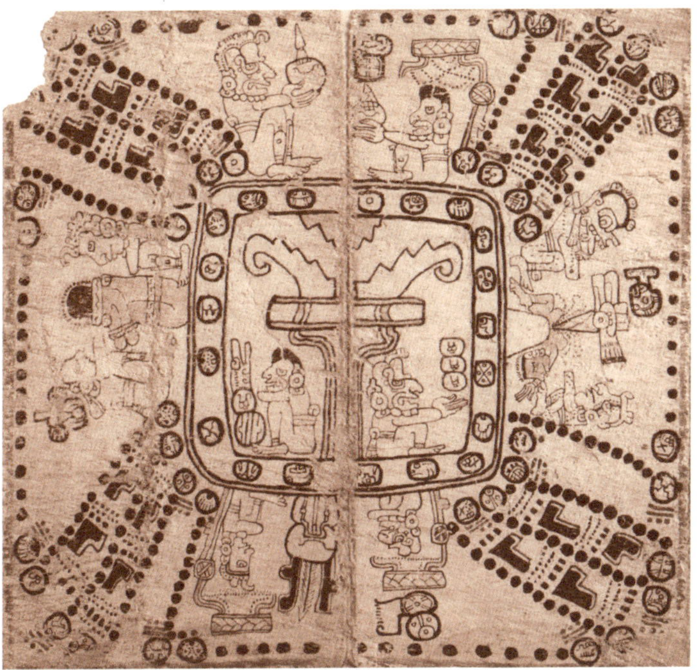

Quadripartite Maya cosmogram painted in the Postclassic Madrid Codex. The so-called World Tree or *axis mundi* (center of the earth) is flanked by two sitting deities and ringed by the Maya hieroglyphs for the twenty days of the 260-day ritual calendar. At each of the four cardinal directions, a pair of deities performs a different sacrificial ritual. The dots and day signs around the four ceremonial scenes take the reader day-by-day through the full 52-year Calendar Round.

from the heart of sky above to the heart of water below; this happened before earth existed, before the first trees and stones arose. By the third day, 3 Ben, everything else had been formed, including all things in the skies, in the seas, and on the earth.

The fourth day, 4 Ix, was when the sun tilted as it rose in the east, separating the skies from the earth. All the god's deeds were made whole on 5 Men, the fifth day. The first candle was shaped on 6 Kib.

It gave light at a time when there was not yet a sun or moon. Day seven of the first winal, 7 Kaban, saw the birth of the world, where we people still did not exist. 8 Etz'nab marked the establishment of the great god's hand and foot upon the earth.

On 9 Kawak, there was the first convocation in Metnal, the ten-layered underworld. Bad people descended to Metnal on 10 Ajaw, before the arrival of God the Father. The next day, 11 Imix, was when

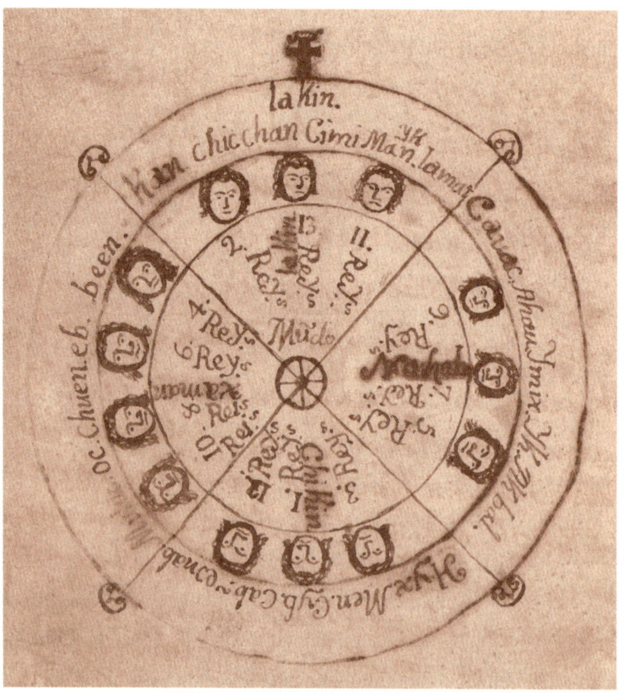

A so-called *k'atun* wheel in the *Chilam Balam of Kaua* (fol. 16r), in which each *k'atun* (7,200-day period) appears as the head of a king. The thirteen *k'atuns* are arranged in groups of three or four according to cardinal direction. The full wheel represents an unbroken count of 93,600 days (7,200 × 13), or just over 256 years.

the god shaped stone and tree. The twelfth day, 12 Ik', marked the birth of wind, the breath of life in which death does not exist. Then, on the thirteenth day, 13 Ak'bal, the great god took water in his hand, wet the surface of the earth, and molded the first human body.

On the fourteenth day, 1 K'an, the god became angered for the first time by evil that had been created. He learned about the evil on the next day, 2 Chikchan, when he glimpsed it with his own eyes. The god forged death for the first time on the sixteenth day, 3 Kimil. What happened on the seventeenth day, 4 Manik, is unclear, but on the eighteenth day, 5 Lamat, there were seven floods, as the oceans overflowed with water. On the final day of the first winal, 6 Muluk, the valleys on the face of the earth were filled in. All this happened during the first winal, when the sun had not yet risen and the world had not yet dawned.

These moments in the shaping of the cosmos, spread over the twenty days of the first winal, occurred because they were ordered by the great god, Our Lord. They took place when nothing was spoken in the skies, when there was no stone or tree on the face of the earth. The first divine beings went and looked at the cosmos themselves, where they found thirteen piles and seven piles, representing the thirteen days of the 260-day calendar and the seven-day week of Judeo-Christian creation, respectively. The great god then declared that the twenty piles were in fact one, a full winal, just like a full human being has ten fingers and ten toes. The god said this even though there was no speech at the time. That was the reason why Yáax Ajaw K'iin, the new Sun god, wished for language to be made, because they did not yet have access to the spoken word, to the tools that would allow them to speak with one another.

The Calendar Round

The pre-colonial Maya commonly paired the 260-day cycle with the 365-day solar year calendar to form a larger cycle that modern scholars have nicknamed the Calendar Round. The 365-day cycle consisted of eighteen "months" of twenty days each, followed by a short transitional period of five days before the new year. The first day of the "month" was known as its "seating," the same term used for a king's accession to the dynastic throne. The Postclassic Yucatec name for the first "month" was Pop ("Mat"), so the first day of the 365-day calendar was the "seating" of Pop, followed by 1 Pop, 2 Pop, and so forth until 19 Pop, the twentieth day. The twenty-first day was the "seating" of the second month, Wo, followed by 1 Wo, 2 Wo, and so on. Thus, in the Yucatec creation myth, the first winal begins with an unnumbered day on which the winal is "born" from U Colel Cab's words and ends on 6 Muluk, the nineteenth numbered day and the twentieth day in the series.

The Calendar Round paired the 260-day and 365-day calendars to record a date by day and month (e.g. 1 Ajaw 3 Pop). This allowed the Maya to precisely track time within a 52-year period, which is the amount of time (18,980 days) between recurrences of any given day–month pairing. The Calendar Round, which is attested as early as the Preclassic period, also gave the Maya the so-called year bearers. For mathematical reasons, only four day signs from the 260-day calendar could ever coincide with the beginning of the 365-day solar year in the Calendar Round. That day sign and its numerical coefficient lent its name to the year that it inaugurated (e.g. the year 1 K'an). Each year bearer was associated with a patron god who was said to mark one of the cosmos' four corners; these are the "Burners" in the Yucatec myth of the creation of the winal.

The Calendar Round was used throughout the Maya world. Over time the alignment of its component cycles has changed, and with it, the identity of the year bearers. Among the Late Postclassic Yucatec, the year bearers were the days K'an, Muluk, Ix, and Kawak. The Dresden Codex documents an earlier Postclassic system in the

The patron deities of the days Eb, Kaban, Ik', and Manik are carried to each cardinal direction, inaugurating a new year. Each god is borne on the back of a mammal with human limbs. In the Postclassic Dresden Codex, Eb, Kaban, Ik', and Manik marked the outgoing solar year, and the new year began on the following day (Ben, Etz'nab, Ak'bal, and Lamat, respectively).

Yucatán peninsula in which Ben, Etz'nab, Ak'bal, and Lamat alternately marked the start of each new solar year. Eb, Kaban, Ik', and Manik are believed to have been the four Classic Maya year bearers, and yet another quartet probably marked the four corners of the Preclassic cosmos. More recent ethnographic studies have also documented variation in year bearers between communities in the Maya highlands, even though the 365-day solar calendar fell out of use there many centuries ago.

So it was, according to the story, that the gods went and stood in front of the heart of the sky. They took each other's hands and looked toward the center of the peninsula as they stood there. It marked the beginning of the four Burners, the four lords called 4 Chikchan, 4 Ok, 4 Men, and 4 Ajaw. The four Burners with their ritual fires, each separated by three-and-a-half winals or 65 days, marked the four corners of the cosmos.

Thus, it is said that the winal was born, and dawn rose over the world. The beginning of time was in the east, where the count of days had its origin. The sky and the earth, the stones and the trees had been shaped because of our Father, the great god. Back then, there was no sky or earth. There was just God, alone in his divinity, who gave birth to all things of the world and gave shape to the heavens.

The myth of the origin of the winal illustrates the fundamental role that time and the calendar played in the composition of the Maya cosmos since its very conception. This principle is by no means specific to the colonial Yucatán peninsula. Evidence from archaeology, art, and hieroglyphic inscriptions demonstrates that, since as early as the Preclassic period, the Maya have conceived of their cosmos as having an essentially quadripartite form, with four corners spaced around a center or *axis mundi*. The same cosmic structure appears in many other Maya creation narratives that have been recorded over the centuries and undergirds the 260-day calendar that was—and, among contemporary highland Maya daykeepers, still is—the foundation of Indigenous divinatory practice.

The Yucatec tale of the winal's creation reflects this relationship in its structure, which goes day-by-day through the twenty days of the winal, just as a daykeeper does in their ritual practice. But the tale from the *Chilam Balam of Chumayel* is not a simple regurgitation of an ancient, fossilized worldview. It very intentionally places a traditional Maya worldview in dialogue with the more recently introduced Catholic religion. At the outset, the mythic song is attributed to a primordial duo consisting of a Yucatec priest, Na Puc Tun, and an enigmatic ritual practitioner mentioned in both the Hebrew Bible and the Christian New Testament, Melchisedek. The account explicitly equates the Christian God (Spanish *Dios*) with the Postclassic Maya Sun god. The latter figure, known in Yucatec as Yáax Ajaw K'iin, was cognate with the Classic Maya Sun god, K'inich Ajaw, a widely worshipped deity with whom divine kings personally identified. The correlation between the Christian God and Ajaw K'iin, in turn, ties

A representation of the thirteen *k'atuns* of the year 1579 in the *Chilam Balam of Chumayel* (fol. 45r).

directly into the calendar because Yucatec, like other Mayan languages, uses the same word (*k'iin*) for "day" and "sun." Explaining the origins of the (Sun) god—in the east, where the sun rises—requires accounting for the origins of time itself, just as this myth does.

As subtle as it may seem to the modern reader, the Yucatec author's incorporation of Judeo-Christian concepts into an otherwise Indigenous narrative makes a clear statement that would have been quite subversive in colonial times. This account of the creation of the first winal suggests that the Maya and Catholic traditions were not only both legitimate but also reconcilable with each other—an attitude that contrasted with the exclusionist position characteristic of Spanish missionaries. The myth reflects a living tradition that was very much shaped by the colonial reality of its anonymous Yucatec singer-narrator.

BROKEN POTS AND WILD BEASTS

Another basic component of Maya cosmogony is a belief in multiple creations. Like other Indigenous Mesoamericans, the Maya have long believed that past iterations of the world were created and subsequently destroyed to make room for humanity. The current universe is only the most recent in a series of creations. Eventually, it will be destroyed to make way for another cosmic renewal, just as prior creations were eliminated to allow ours to come into being. Maya sources do not agree on precisely how many creations preceded ours, nor on the nature of the beings that populated them. But they are consistent in locating prior creations' downfall in moral shortcoming, particularly in the inhabitants' failure to properly serve the gods and ancestors. The basic principle of reciprocity between humans and other-than-human beings, including gods, animals, and material objects, defines tales of earlier creations' apocalyptic demise.

Accounts of the rise and fall of previous creations have been documented across the Maya region, from the western highlands of Chiapas to the lowlands of Belize. The oldest, and by far the most detailed, version is recorded in the *Popol Vuh*. It describes the previous creation as inhabited by people who were quite a lot like us: They walked on two legs, communed with each other, spent their day growing maize and other crops in the milpa, and lived in houses filled with the pots, grindstones, and stone hearths typical of any Maya household. But unlike humans today, who are composed of flesh and blood, the men of this creation had been fashioned from the wood of the coral tree, known as *tz'ite'* in K'iche'. The women, in turn, had been shaped from reeds like those that the Maya have long used for braiding mats.

The *Popol Vuh*

The contents of the famous K'iche' manuscript known as the *Popol Vuh* (literally "Mat Book") date back at least to Postclassic times. They were first recorded as an alphabetic text in the area of Santa Cruz del Quiché in the Department of El Quiché, Guatemala, during the mid-sixteenth century. The lengthy manuscript, which was compiled by members of a K'iche' lineage known as the Kaweq, contains a wealth of information about highland Maya cosmology, mythology, and history. Its elegant language and intricate structure reflect the richness of traditional Maya poetics. The oldest surviving copy, which Dominican friar Francisco Ximénez transcribed and partially translated into Spanish, dates to the early eighteenth century. Since 1911, Ximénez's manuscript has been housed in the Newberry Library in Chicago, Illinois.

Eventually, the creators became dissatisfied because the people were unable to speak to or worship them properly. The creation was doomed because the wooden men and reed women could not perform the rituals necessary to sustain the gods and ancestors and, ultimately, the cosmos itself. Dismayed that the people whom they had created could not reciprocate the respect and nurturing that they had invested in making them, the creators realized that they had no choice but to wipe out their creation and start over again from scratch.

One day, the creators obscured the sun, causing darkness to fall on the earth during daytime. Suddenly, the sky opened, and a devastating deluge of pine resin poured forth like black rain. The diluvium did not ravage the physical world as much as it turned society upside down. Chaos ensued. What the wooden and reed people had taken

An eclipse event is represented by a serpent eating the sun in the Postclassic Dresden Codex (p. 60b).

Postclassic Maya deities Chahk (left) and Chak Chel (right) pour rain from upturned jars. Madrid Codex (fol. 30a).

for granted as basic facts of existence were inverted, and they found themselves trapped in a terrifying new reality.

Domestic animals that had lived peacefully by their masters' sides turned upon them. With newfound voices, they chastised the people for the mistreatment that they had suffered. "Pain you have caused us," the turkeys cried. "You ate us. Therefore it will be you that we will eat now." The dogs complained of hunger, asking "Why was it that you didn't give us our food? … You raised sticks against us to beat us while you ate .... This day, therefore, you shall try the teeth that are in our mouths. We shall eat you!"

Household possessions became animated, too, and were even endowed with the power of speech. Like the animals, they threatened to take revenge on the people who had abused them. Grindstones scolded the reed women for having pulverized corn on their faces, day after day. They menaced their former masters, saying, "This day you shall feel our strength. We shall grind you like maize. We shall grind up your flesh." Hearthstones rose up against the people, smashing their heads with retaliatory force. Cooking pots vowed to

---

"The Revolt of the Objects"

Although the details of the *Popol Vuh*'s account of the destruction of a previous creation are unique, the narrative motif of objects and domesticated animals revolting against their human masters at a long-ago time when the sun disappeared is not. Variations on the theme have been identified from the Great Plains of the modern-day United States down to South America. Scenes painted on pottery and in wall murals during the first century BCE by artists from the Moche civilization in coastal Peru show animals and legged objects pursuing humans and taking them captive. A short myth documented in the Peruvian highlands during the early seventeenth century reads much like the *Popol Vuh* account, except that the animals rising up alongside the grinding stones are llamas.

The Zuni Tribe in what is now New Mexico has a similar story in the form of a prophecy instead of a tale about the primordial past. In an account from the late twentieth century, the Zuni foretell an apocalyptic future in which the sun ceases to shine, rain no longer falls, the air becomes toxic, and domestic objects and animals consume the people. It is impossible to determine whether these

---

The Postclassic Maize god is attacked by a vulture and dogs. Madrid Codex (fol. 87a).

myths about the so-called Revolt of the Objects share a common origin or instead reflect the outcome of long-term exchanges of ideas reaching back into ancient times. They do, however, suggest that the Maya were not unique among Indigenous Americans in understanding their creation and control over resources and the environment as earned, rather than as a given.

A scene on a Moche vessel from coastal Peru depicts an array of animals, ornaments, headdresses, weapons, and even a spindle chasing humans and taking captives.

burn them, just like they abused the pots in the fire: "Our mouths and our faces are sooty. You were forever throwing us upon the fire and burning us. Although we felt no pain, you now shall try it."

The wooden and reed people thus found themselves in a desperate fight with the very beings and things on which their lives had depended. It was a fight that they would ultimately lose. They tried to escape the wrath of the objects and animals by climbing onto the roofs of their houses, but the structures crumbled beneath them. The trees refused to let them scale their branches to safety. Even caves closed their openings, denying entry to the doomed people. In the end, the wooden and reed people could not avoid their apocalyptic fate.

The creators did not eliminate the wooden and reed people entirely, however. The *Popol Vuh* authors suggest that these earlier people may be ancestors of the spider monkeys that still populate the subtropical canopies of the Maya lowlands. Still, the fallen figures clearly did not have the authority and privilege that they had enjoyed before. The creators populated their next version of the world with people shaped from maize dough—the Maya themselves. The maize people's devotion to the gods and ancestors has sustained this most recent creation into the present.

Like other Maya accounts of a primordial apocalypse, the *Popol Vuh* tale of a prior creation is set in an unspecified time in the distant past. The implication is that the same disruptions that affected much earlier peoples, in a world physically and spiritually analogous to ours, could be triggered again by transgressions against the established world order. At the same time, the devastating failure of previous creations to uphold their obligations to the gods provided an opportunity for renewal. Without the shortcomings of these past peoples, the creators would not have forged humanity and our world as we know it today. Death and destruction are necessary preludes to rebirth in a cosmic cycle that stretches beyond the span of individual or generational memory.

A RABBIT ROBS THE LORD OF THE UNDERWORLD

A variation on this theme of cosmogenic correction can be found in the tale of the rabbit who robs the lord of the underworld. The story portrays a confrontation between light and darkness in a primordial age before our ancestors walked the earth. It also represents a rare instance of a narrative that has been handed down to us in Classic Maya hieroglyphic texts. Although fragmented and difficult to decipher in sections, it records a fascinating and at times hilarious disagreement involving two prominent gods and a rabbit, the story's unlikely hero. Readers familiar with other mythological traditions may recognize in the wily creature shades of the trickster that stars in many other cultures. Figures like Br'er Rabbit among Africans and African-Americans, the coyote or the crow in Native North America, Puck in English folklore, or the Classic Maya rabbit reflect a cross-cultural human concern with authority and social norms, and the alternately destructive and productive consequences of defying them.

Before our world was created, the hieroglyphic sources tell us, an elderly god governed the cosmos. (His name has not been deciphered, so we refer to him here by a nickname, God L.) Wealthy and powerful beyond measure, the aged sovereign reigned over a universe that he kept under a perpetual cover of darkness. In this

God L, clad in his typical fringed cape and avian hat and smoking a cigar, sits on his throne (right) as he receives bundled tribute from six subordinate gods sitting before him (left).

primordial age, there was no sun, and the first people had not yet been created. In a dim palace filled with riches, God L sat atop a throne draped with a jaguar pelt whose black spots resembled the dark patches on his wrinkled face. He ruled over the other gods, and the tribute that his divine subjects paid to him only added to the old god's already substantial wealth.

Among the members of God L's entourage was a rabbit. This modest creature's tasks in God L's court included managing the aged lord's many riches, such as his elaborate headdresses, painted books, and flint effigies. These treasures were stored on a legendary mountain known as K'inuwitz, which stood amid a watery landscape called Pihpa'. After having spent much of his life serving God L, however, the rabbit grew tired of the lord's self-importance, and yearned to humble the old god.

Ceramic figurine from Jaina Island, Campeche, Mexico, of a young goddess with a rabbit.

On the day 13 Ok, in the month 18 Ik'at, the rabbit finally had an opportunity to take action against the old underworld lord. God L met with Bolon Yookte', the artisan in K'inuwitz charged with creating the old god's ornate headdresses. The pair traveled together to a place of blossoming foliage, which may have been called Sak Ajsunaal Ho' Nikte'. God L wanted to retrieve his newest hat, which had been completed there just six days earlier. The occasion also presented an excuse to visit the Moon goddess, God L's favorite consort. The young lunar goddess was also a close companion of

A portrait of the Moon goddess (left) and God L (right) facing each other in the Postclassic Dresden Codex (p. 23c).

the disgruntled rabbit, however. It was this relationship that would lead to God L's demise.

When God L arrived at the Moon goddess's residence, the rabbit was already there. As per usual, the rabbit helped the old god undress, removing his hat, cape, and other finery. This time, however, the rabbit decided to finally humiliate the old god. While God L was with the Moon goddess, the rabbit snuck into the room where the underworld lord's finery was stored. The first target was the signature hat, topped with a fierce owl, that always covered God L's balding head like a ferocious crown. The rabbit also made off with the aged lord's precious jade necklace, elegantly embroidered cape, and fine serpentine scepter.

While the Moon goddess was still entertaining God L, the rabbit fled with the stolen goods to a distant mountain. It was not long, however, before God L went to get dressed and discovered that several

God L kneels before the Moon goddess and the rabbit, with four other gods standing behind the old lord. The rabbit holds God L's fringed cape.

of his most prized possessions were missing. His initial confusion turned to consternation and then rage when he learned—the sources do not tell us how—who had orchestrated the theft. Perhaps the rabbit had divulged the plot to an untrustworthy source, or someone at the Moon goddess's court had spotted the leporid in action and reported it to the old lord.

As soon as God L heard the news, he rushed away to the mountain where the rabbit was said to be hiding with the stolen treasures. As the rabbit had pilfered all his finery, the disheveled lord had to set off in complete nakedness. Even his sparse hair, normally hidden beneath his luxurious hat, was unkempt and stood upright in tufts atop his uncrowned head.

The rabbit did not seem surprised when God L appeared at the base of his mountain hideout. Seeing the underworld lord standing naked below, the rabbit launched a string of insults at him. "Go hit your head, go smell your piss! Your penis and balls are just mesh!" God L was taken aback, unaccustomed to being addressed crudely. Meanwhile, a snake had emerged from the caves at the base of the mountain, lifting its head up to the humbled underworld lord and blocking the path up to the rabbit's den.

Desperate to retrieve his clothing, God L bent his right arm across his chest and rested his right hand on his left shoulder, a standard gesture of deference among the Classic Maya. God L could only implore the mischievous thief from the base of the mountain. "If my ancestors could see this … where are my clothes, where is my image?" he lamented. The rabbit responded by brandishing the purloined items and taunting the humiliated old man from atop the mountain. It became clear to God L that the rabbit was not going to return the items so easily. He also knew that he was ill-equipped for a fight.

The rabbit taunts God L from atop an animated mountain. A volute or "speech scroll" connects the rabbit's mouth to the words that he is speaking to the naked lord, while God L's statement to the rabbit floats above the old god's head.

Reluctantly, the aged god decided to plead his case before the Sun god, K'inich Ajaw, hoping that the lord of daylight would understand his complaint against the little mammal. Thus, God L appeared before the Sun god, who was seated upon his own plush, jaguar pelt-covered throne atop another high mountain, known as Chij Tuun Witz ("Deer-Stone Mountain"). Clad in nothing more than a thin loincloth and a netted headscarf that he had hastily scrounged up on his way to Chij Tuun Witz, the old lord went down on one knee before the Sun god over whom he, the god of darkness, had long ruled. To emphasize his complete submission, God L even crossed both arms across his chest, putting each hand on the opposite shoulder.

"Look," the underworld god insisted, "it was the rabbit who took my insignias, my clothing, my tribute!" Burning with embarrassment as he knelt, God L watched from the corner of one eye as another rattlesnake slithered toward him, tongue outstretched, discouraging the uninvited visitor from ascending any closer to K'inich Ajaw.

The Sun god did not appear particularly moved by God L's plight. Still, he seemed to understand the hardship that the old lord was suffering. He assured the visitor that his stolen possessions would be recovered and returned to him. In fact, K'inich Ajaw said, one of his associates had already captured the rabbit in a place called Nik Ha'al, where the thief had been trying to sell off the booty.

What God L did not realize was that the Sun god already knew about the robbery. Not only that, but by the time God L approached the Sun god, the rabbit had left his mountaintop hideout to seek refuge elsewhere—namely, with K'inich Ajaw himself. Having stashed the stolen goods out of God L's reach, the rabbit crouched behind the powerful lord of light. Hidden from view, the rabbit eavesdropped as the underworld lord complained bitterly about what the devious creature had done to him.

The Sun god's alliance with the rabbit was no coincidence. It was the rabbit's humiliation of the underworld lord, in fact, that broke God L's uncontested power. By petitioning K'inich Ajaw and accepting his aid to retrieve the stolen treasures, God L ceded some of his authority to the lord of light. Before the rabbit's theft, K'inich Ajaw

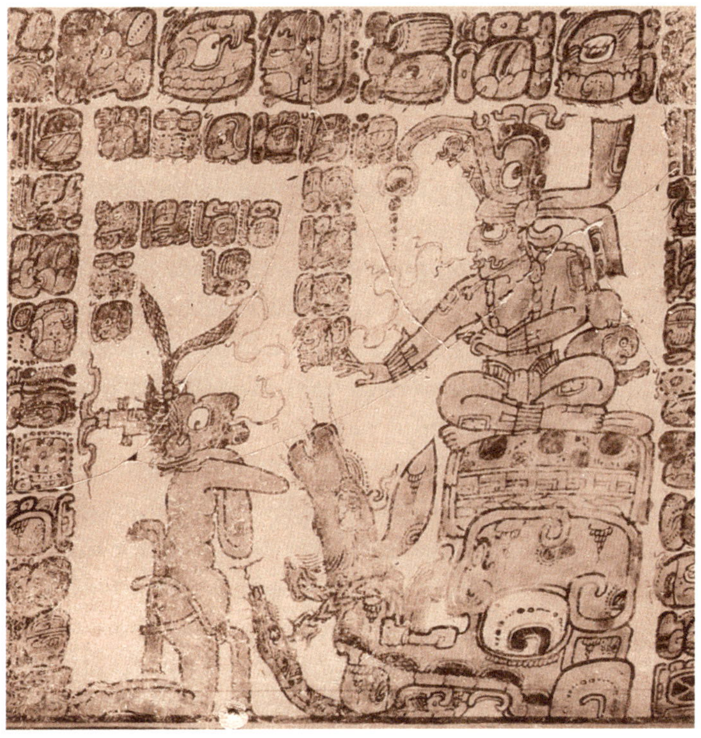

God L kneels before the enthroned Sun god to plead his case. The rabbit eavesdrops on their exchange from his hiding place behind the Sun god's left thigh. Again, note the speech scrolls connecting God L and the Sun god's mouths to their respective statements.

had been forced to live in hiding, subject to the underworld lord's whims. After the rabbit's theft, he could reign over the universe alongside God L, regularly breaking through the old god's darkness to brighten the universe with his light.

This Classic Maya myth accounts for the triumph of light over darkness during a time before humans had been created, when life on earth was not yet defined by the planetary rhythms that the people take for granted. God L appears as an out-of-touch, self-indulgent ruler whose power is based on undeserved wealth. The rabbit, a servant in the underworld lord's court, would seem to have no chance to overthrow the lofty master. Unlike the aged deity, however, the rabbit is clever, observant, and daring. Familiar with God L's habits, the rabbit surprises the old lord when he least expects it.

The plot succeeds not only because of a well-laid plan but also because its mastermind has cultivated powerful allies from whom to seek help when needed. Importantly, the rabbit seeks refuge and assistance with the Sun god, K'inich Ajaw. The solar deity's capacity to bring light to the world offers a complementary counterbalance to the darkness of God L and the underworld, which had dominated the cosmos until that point. The rabbit's takedown of God L paves the way for the origin of the sun and the moon and the daily rhythms of the sky as we know it today.

2

SUN AND MOON

In the beginning, the Maya cosmos was dark, watery, and empty. Even as the gods gradually filled it with their creations, the sun and the moon did not immediately occupy the roles that they fulfill now. As we saw in Chapter 1, darkness predominated; light was limited, and when it did shine, it was not the light of the sun. The sun and its nocturnal counterpart, the moon, had to come into their own over the course of earlier creations. This chapter recounts three of the many Maya stories that explain how the sun, moon, and other planetary bodies arrived at their now-familiar places in the heavens' daily cycle. The first is set during an earlier creation, before the maize people (the Maya) were shaped, when the sky was feebly lit and dominated by a prideful god whose influence was greater than his merit. Its protagonists are perhaps the most famous Maya ancestors today, the brothers Junajpu' and Xb'alanke'. While early images of the so-called Hero Twins have survived on Classic Maya ceramics, most of what is known about the fraternal pair—including their role in allowing light to illuminate the sky—is recorded in the *Popol Vuh*.

BALANCING THE SKIES: A BLOWGUNNER AND A BIRD

The first myth takes place at a time when, according to the *Popol Vuh*, the faces of the sun and the moon were still dimmed, so that

A Classic Maya bowl with a lid in the form of a scarlet macaw.

their feeble light did not fully illuminate the surface of the earth. There was no brightness to distinguish day from night. But there was one who considered himself the bringer of light for the world. His name was Wuqub' Kaqix ("Seven Macaw"), and he sat upon a gold and silver throne high in the sky. When he left his perch to soar on feathered wings above the people and other animals below, his precious jewel eyes, polished jade teeth, and fine plumage reflected what little light illuminated this early creation. Thus, the great bird floated above the earth like a bright star.

Wuqub' Kaqix fancied himself to be both the sun and the moon because of his brilliance. He proclaimed to anyone who would listen that he was not just a giver of light but a seer, endowed with vision that reached to the farthest corner of the earth. So, Wuqub' Kaqix said, he knew everything that was happening under the sky.

Preening his silky feathers and puffing out his chest, the great macaw was prideful beyond measure. Yet Wuqub' Kaqix was not truly all-seeing or all-knowing, nor did he shine as brightly in the world as he imagined. He had two sons, Sipakna and Kab'raqan. Their pride was so great that it did not leave room for people to walk the earth. In the end, Wuqub' Kaqix's insatiable hubris would be his downfall.

Along with the pretentious macaw and his sons, the inhabitants of this prior creation included twin boys named Junajpu' and Xb'alanke'. Like the creator gods, Junajpu' and Xb'alanke' were offended by the arrogance of Wuqub' Kaqix and his brood. The boys knew that the trio were merely gods like them. Together, the brothers hatched a plot to humble the glittering macaw and his noisy, disruptive sons by stripping them of the distinctions of which they were so proud.

The twins first targeted Wuqub' Kaqix himself. Like everyone else, they knew that the macaw's favorite food was nance, a small, round fruit with golden-white flesh. Every day, he alighted on the top of a great nance tree, shaking its branches to dislodge the yellow pearls that he would immediately eat from the ground.

One day, the twins staked out the tree to await the great bird's arrival. When the macaw landed on his usual branch, Junajpu' took a deep breath and blew forcefully into his blowgun. The pellet streaked upward through the air and struck Wuqub' Kaqix in the jaw. The bird cried out in pained surprise as he fell from the treetop, landing hard on the ground.

Junajpu' leaped out of the brothers' hiding place behind the tree's thick leaves. He wanted to seize the wounded bird and remove his jewels and precious metals before he could escape. But Wuqub' Kaqix recovered from the blow more quickly than the brothers had anticipated. When Junajpu' approached, the macaw ripped off the

K'an Mo' Hix, father of the Late Classic king K'inich Janaab Pakal II of Palenque in Chiapas, Mexico, appears in a posthumous portrait on his son's sarcophagus as a flourishing nance tree.

boy's arm with his strong beak. After wrenching the arm free from Junajpu's shoulder and picking up his broken jaw, Wuqub' Kaqix took off for home.

Arriving at home, Wuqub' Kaqix was met by his wife, who was startled by her husband's disfigured, ruffled appearance. She asked what had happened and what he had brought home with him. Wuqub' Kaqix answered that two rascals had shot him down and dislocated his jaw. He did not know who the culprits were, but his mouth and especially his teeth radiated with pain from the blow. He told his wife that he would keep the arm of one of his attackers, storing it above the hearth until the demons returned to claim the severed limb.

Meanwhile, the thwarted twins returned home to consult with the first grandmother, Saq Nima Sis ("Great White Coati"), and the first grandfather, Saq Nim Aq ("Great White Peccary"). As their names suggest, both gods' heads were crowned with white hair, and their aged bodies doubled over when they walked. The elders listened as the boys recounted the confrontation with Wuqub' Kaqix. The twins asked for help in recovering Junajpu's stolen arm and in executing the new plan that they had to finally defeat the large bird who had seized it. "Very well," agreed Saq Nima Sis and Saq Nim Aq. The four set out together to meet Wuqub' Kaqix.

When the small party arrived at Wuqub' Kaqix's home, they found the macaw seated on his golden and silver throne, wailing in agony about his jaw and teeth. He asked the strangers where they were from, using informal language to express his sense of superiority. The first grandparents responded just as the twins had instructed, addressing the lord with honorific speech and saying that they were

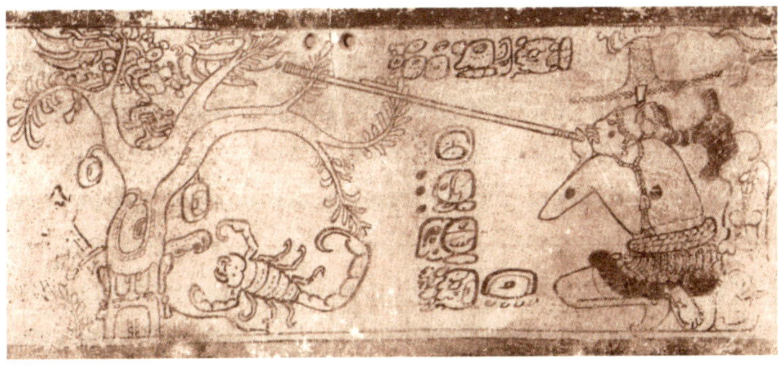

A blowgunner takes aim at a bird in a tree as a scorpion looks on. The hieroglyphic text under the blowgun identifies the target as a hybrid of the old God D and the so-called Principal Bird Deity, the Classic Maya counterpart of Wuqub' Kaqix. The same text, plus the spots on his skin, indicate that the hunter is none other than Junajpu', whom the Classic Maya called Juun Ajaw.

On a stela from Izapa, Chiapas, Mexico, a Late Preclassic version of the Principal Bird Deity perches atop a staff while a smaller bird sits in a crocodile-tree nearby. The human figure below the staff bleeds where his left forearm has been ripped off. The severed limb dangles limply from serpent jaws that emerge from the Principal Bird Deity's abdomen.

mere healers. When Wuqub' Kaqix inquired about the small boys behind them, Saq Nima Sis and Saq Nim Aq answered that they were their grandchildren, whom they had taken in out of pity and fed with table scraps. Thus, the first grandparents did not reveal Junajpu' and Xb'alanke's identities.

By this point, Wuqub' Kaqix was weak from the toothache and felt that he was about to faint. He begged the aged visitors for compassion and aid, asking what medicines they could make to relieve his suffering. Modestly, they replied that they only treated damaged teeth, injured eyes, and broken bones. "Very well," Wuqub' Kaqix said. "Cure, then, my teeth, for truly they ache constantly, and I can no longer bear it. I cannot sleep because of them, and the same goes for my eyes." He told them that two demons had shot him with a blowgun and that he had not been able to eat or rest since then because the pain was so great.

"Very well, thou lord," agreed Saq Nima Sis and Saq Nim Aq. They warned that they would have to remove and replace the bird's broken teeth to relieve the pain. Wuqub' Kaqix protested, obstinate even with a toothache. "It is perhaps not a good thing that my teeth come out, for it is only because of them that I am lord. My teeth, along with my eyes, are my finery." In the moment, though, the injured bird's discomfort was stronger than his pride. When the aged healers assured him that they would replace his jade teeth with ground bone, he consented.

Reconstruction of an Early Classic stucco macaw from the ballcourt at Copan, Honduras. Note the serpent head that protrudes from the macaw's groin and clenches a human arm in its jaws.

Thus, the first grandparents removed Wuqub' Kaqix's shining, broken teeth. One by one, they plucked each blue-green jewel from the bird's wounded jaw. But instead of replacing the teeth with ground bone, as they had promised, they inserted kernels of white maize, as they had been instructed by Junajpu' and Xb'alanke'. They treated Wuqub' Kaqix's eyes by removing the precious metals that had made them gleam. The macaw was left with only a beady, black eye surrounded by a bare patch of white feathers. Thus, Saq Nima Sis and Saq Nim Aq relieved Wuqub' Kaqix's suffering. In their deception, the first grandmother and first grandfather also relieved the vain bird of his finery, the source of his self-importance.

Later, after the humbled Wuqub' Kaqix died, Junajpu' retrieved his missing limb. The twins repositioned it in his shoulder, and the socket healed to hold the arm as before. That is how, with the help of the first grandmother and first grandfather, Junajpu' and Xb'alanke' freed the creation from the prideful bird who had claimed to be its light. Their deed finally created room for the sun and the moon to shine.

Complementarity has been fundamental to the Maya cosmos since its inception and often finds expression in dualism, the pairing of two opposing characters or forces—male–female, hot–cold, or young–old, for instance—that balance and supplement each other. In this adventure, the boys Junajpu' and Xb'alanke' take it upon themselves to humble a fellow god who is so pompous that he fancies himself bright enough to illuminate the young sky. The brothers go up against this more powerful opponent, who triumphs in their initial encounter. As a rich, strong, self-aggrandizing character, Wuqub' Kaqix has all the trappings of a Maya anti-hero. Unlike the poor Hero Twins, he wears gleaming jewels, preens his feathers, and

An image of the Postclassic Maya Sun god holding a spear-thrower (*atlatl*) in front of a temple. Maya Codex of Mexico (p. 5).

sits on a shiny throne. The material contrast is reinforced during the meeting between Wuqub' Kaqix and the first grandparents, who describe themselves as humble healers of modest means.

Ultimately, the twins successfully restore the balance necessary to maintain the Maya cosmos. The *Popol Vuh* authors make clear that Wuqub' Kaqix's power and wealth are not in themselves problematic; they become faults because of the pride that the macaw takes in them. As in the Classic Maya narrative of the ostentatious God L (see Chapter 1), Wuqub' Kaqix's power was not justified because it was based only on the macaw's material riches, rather than great deeds or cleverness. The language describing Wuqub' Kaqix's inflated sense of self explicitly associates pride with filth, deception, ugliness, and evil. It thus comes as no surprise that this vice leads to the macaw's humiliation. From the narrator's perspective, Wuqub' Kaqix loses power and wealth that he had never deserved to wield.

THE ORIGINS OF THE SUN AND THE MOON

The basic principles of balance and complementarity are at the heart of Maya myths about the origins of the sun and the moon, the planetary bodies that reign over night and day and determine the basic rhythms of life on earth. Two such tales are reproduced here. The first originates from the Tseltal community of Bachajón in Chiapas, Mexico, during the late twentieth century; the second is compiled from tales documented among Q'eqchi' speakers in San Antonio, Toledo District, Belize, and Senahú, Alta Verapaz, Guatemala, in the early to mid-twentieth century. Like all myths in this book, they represent samples from a mythological range or variations on a common Maya concern with two of humanity's most enduring heavenly companions.

Blue Sun and Youngest of the Family

A long time ago, the Tseltal story goes, there was an old woman who gave birth to two sons. The eldest was known as Blue Sun; the other was named Youngest of the Family. Every day, the pair walked to work together, and Blue Sun killed Youngest of the Family, cutting off his head and hiding it.

A Late Classic stucco portrait of the Sun god from Palenque. Note the deity's distinctive T-shaped tooth and the linear marks on his forehead, which indicate brilliance or shininess.

Every day, when Blue Sun arrived home alone, their mother asked her older son where his younger brother was. Each time, Blue Sun responded, "I don't know; he stayed behind to play somewhere, I don't know where." Sometimes Blue Sun came home a little earlier; at other times, it would already be dark. But he always returned home without his brother.

Still, Youngest of the Family would not die. Day after day, his body would reassemble after he was killed, and the boy would return to life. Blue Sun sometimes threw his brother's head into a hole and

The Color of the Chol Sun

A similar Chol myth from Palenque, Chiapas, Mexico, is more specific with its color associations, describing the older brother as the white (*säsäk*) sun and the younger brother as the green (*yäjyäx*) sun. Mayan languages do not make a native distinction between the colors called "green" and "blue" in English. Instead, they refer to the green–blue spectrum with a single word, usually something like *yax* or *rax* depending on the language. The younger brother may be described in the Chol account as the "green" sun because of the color's associations with new life, like a sprouting plant. Why the older brother specifically appears as white is less clear, but it may reflect the color's traditional correlation with the cardinal direction north, or the zenith of the sun's daily transit—the point at which its light and heat are strongest.

cut the decapitated body into pieces, thinking that perhaps that way his brother would stay dead. But then wasps and bees would come, gather the pieces, and put them back together.

One day, Youngest of the Family visited their elderly mother as she was spinning thread next to a pile of cottonseeds. He grabbed a handful of the seeds and left. He walked into the forest, where he tossed the seeds into an old tree trunk. The seeds transformed into a beehive, full of honeycombs dripping with sweet syrup. Seeing this, Youngest of the Family called to his older brother to come with him to eat honey from the hive. Blue Sun dismissed him, thinking that he was merely joking. But Youngest of the Family insisted that there was honey in the old tree. "Fine," Blue Sun relented, "let's go then. But if we don't find any honey, you know what will happen to you—you won't return alive."

The brothers set off together into the woods. Upon reaching the old tree, Blue Sun saw that there was, indeed, a beehive with honey far above among the branches. He scaled the tree while Youngest of the Family watched from below. When Blue Sun reached the hive, he began scraping honey out of the hive and eating it right there with his hands. "Give me some, too!" Youngest of the Family cried up from the ground. But Blue Sun kept eating the honey in the tree. Finally, he scooped out a piece of honeycomb from the hive. "Where are you?" he called down to his younger brother. "Go stand out in the open."

Once he could see Youngest of the Family, Blue Sun threw down the honeycomb, which hit his brother on the head. "Ouch!" the junior sibling cried out. "That hurt!" He took the piece in his hand, drove a sharp palmwood stick through it, and pushed it into the

The god Itzamnaaj conducts a ceremony in front of a beehive in a Postclassic image from the Madrid Codex's Beekeeping Almanac (fol. 106a).

Late Classic stucco portrait from Tonina, Chiapas, Mexico, of a supernatural gopher holding a bundle. The hieroglyphs next to the bundle identify the creature as K'an Baah Ch'o Xaman ("Yellow Gopher-Rat North").

base of the tree. Youngest of the Family asked for more honeycomb, and Blue Sun tossed down another piece, which also landed on his head before he planted it at the foot of the tree.

With his small machete, Youngest of the Family began hacking at the base of the tree. From his perch up in the old tree, Blue Sun heard the commotion. He shouted down at his brother, "What are you doing? Don't cut down the tree while I'm up here!"

"What would I fell you with?" Youngest of the Family responded, holding up his machete to show his brother how little it was. "Would I fell you with this machete of mine?" He asked his brother to please give him more honeycomb, and Blue Sun dropped more bits for him. Youngest of the Family put them along the base of the tree, just as he had done with the others.

Suddenly, a gopher appeared and began gnawing at the base of the tree. In fact, the gopher's teeth were the hard palmwood sticks that the boy had stuck into the beeswax. (They say that it is because of Youngest of the Family that gophers have no skeleton. They are merely made of beeswax—that is why we are able to eat their bones, but not their teeth or claws.) The gopher worked around the base of the tree, cutting through the roots and the trunk.

The tree fell over, killing Blue Sun, who was crushed under the trunk and branches. His body broke into many pieces. The large ones became the deer, the lowland paca, the boar, and other big mammals. Smaller fragments turned into the birds flying in the sky, as did his clotted blood. Thus, Blue Sun's death marked the animals' creation.

After Blue Sun and the tree had fallen, Youngest of the Family returned home. When he arrived, their aged mother asked him, "Where is your older brother? You never arrive home first." "I don't

Tortillas and a Pig in San Juan Chamula

A related myth from San Juan Chamula, a Tsotsil Maya town in Chiapas, deviates significantly from the Tseltal account at this point. According to the Tsotsil version, the younger brother confessed to causing his older sibling's death, but refused to claim responsibility. "It's really his own fault," he insisted, "for he gave me no honey to eat. He gave me nothing but the chewed-up honeycomb. That's why I got mad and knocked the tree over. He was perched in the tree when it fell into a gully."

The boys' horrified mother, the moon, began to cry and chastised him, saying that only her older son had known how to work and tended to the maize field that fed them, and that they would die without him. To console her, the junior child assured their mother that he would bring his older brother back to life, though he defended once again his decision to fell the tree with his brother in it. He asked his mother to prepare three *memela* tortillas—plump, toasted corncakes covered with toppings—before he set off back into the forest.

Memelas in hand, the second brother followed the path back to the ravine where his dead sibling was lying face-up on the ground. He took the memelas and positioned them on his brother's nose. Immediately, the dead boy woke up, turned into a pig, and began grunting. The two set off for home, the pig leading the way.

When the pair arrived back at the house, the younger brother told his mother with some satisfaction that her oldest son had returned home. Astonished, their mother admonished her younger child again. "Why did you play this wicked trick on your older brother?" "It's his own fault," her second son retorted. "He didn't give me honey to eat. But I did revive him, Mother." His older brother, the pig, simply grunted. That is why, the Tsotsil myth concludes, the pig's snout looks like a hoe and is round, because it was made from three memelas. Its snout is also the reason why the pig is so good at foraging in the dirt and digging up worms.

know," the boy answered, "He stayed behind somewhere, I don't know where." "You probably killed him," the old woman said. "No," Youngest of the Family responded, "why would I kill my older brother?" Their mother continued waiting for Blue Sun to return and became anxious when he did not appear, wondering where he was.

"Don't be sad," Youngest of the Family told her. "Shell some corn, and animals will come soon. When they do, make sure that you feed them immediately, and choose the ones you like, so that they can become your pets." So, the old woman began shelling maize, and indeed, animals began to emerge from the forest. She gave them some kernels to eat. Just as the boy had advised her, she also took a few of the animals that she liked into her arms. "Don't laugh at them," Youngest of the Family cautioned, "for if you laugh at them

Portrait of a lunar deity holding a rabbit incised on an obsidian flake from Uaxactun, Petén, Guatemala.

Domesticated and Wild Animals in Palenque

According to the Chol version of this story, the animals returned with the younger brother when he went back to the house instead of arriving later, and they were not frightened away by laughter. Instead, it was the tears and sobbing of the boys' mother, the moon, that startled them. Some were scared so badly that they fled all the way back to the forest. According to the Chol myth, all wild pigs, pacas, deer, and armadillos that now live in the forest once belonged to us humans, but when the sun's mother began to cry, half of the animals ran away. Only those that stayed behind, including chickens and pigs, still live among the people today.

while you hold them, their tails will come off, and they will escape, leaving you only with their tails."

As the old woman held the animals, they began jumping around, and she could not help laughing with amusement. But the animals were afraid of being laughed at, so they started to run away. As they fled, their tails fell off into the old woman's hands. That is why the deer, the boar, the rabbit, and the lowland paca eat maize, but do not have tails. Still, the old woman was able to hold onto the rabbit. She, our heavenly mother, still grasps the rabbit today, for she is the moon. They say that one can see the rabbit standing with her in the center of the moon.

A Heavenly Triangle: The Sun, His Brother, and the Moon

A Q'eqchi' myth recounts how, early in the history of the world, when the planetary bodies were just being established, the sun built a home for himself and his wife, the moon, in the sky. The sun invited his older brother, who had declined to take a wife of his own, to live with the newlyweds. Tension arose, however, after the brother and the moon fell in love at first sight.

Whenever the sun left to hunt, his brother would remain behind with the moon. She then showered affection on her husband when he returned, so that he would not become aware of her betrayal. It did not take long, however, before the jealous sun realized that his brother and wife were having an affair. He did not say anything about his suspicions, instead hatching a plan to catch them in the act and punish them for their deceit.

One day, when the sun was out for a walk, he encountered a turkey and asked for bile from its gallbladder. Continuing along the

A Postclassic Maya portrait of the Sun god as a warrior, on a jade pendant recovered from the Sacred Cenote at Chichen Itza, Yucatán, Mexico.

road, he came upon a chicken and asked for some of its gall, too. He stopped by the home of an elderly lady and asked her to make a tamale with the bile from the birds, chili powder, and red annatto paste, all wrapped in maize dough. On the way back home, the sun cradled the tamale under his arm to cook it as he walked.

When he returned to the house, the sun found his brother and wife sitting together. He pulled out the freshly cooked tamale and offered it to the disloyal couple. They accepted the food, splitting it between each other. As soon as they took the first bite, they began retching and choking. Their eyes watered from the chili's heat, and their mouths burned with the tamale's revolting, bile-infused flavor. They emptied all the water jars in the house, but still could not get rid of the bad taste in their mouths.

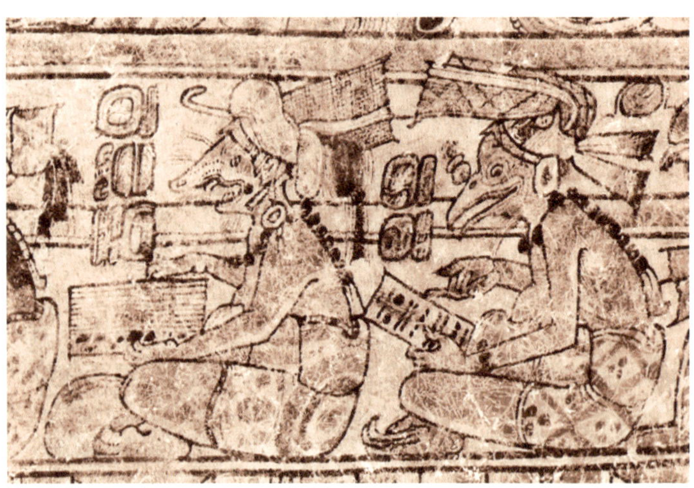

Portraits on a Late Classic Maya ceramic vase of an opossum holding a closed barkpaper codex (left) and a vulture reading a sheet of hieroglyphic numbers (right).

Speaking harshly, with words and a tone that he had never used with his companion, the sun's brother ordered the moon to go outside to fetch them more water. The moon found an empty jar and set out to refill it at the nearby river, but—feeling sick from the tamale and hurt by her lover's rude address—instead of filling the jar and heading home, she sat down on the bank and began to cry when she arrived at the edge of the water.

A vulture noticed the young woman sitting alone in sorrow and swooped down to see what the matter was. Between sobs, the moon said that she hated her husband, who was mistreating her. She wished the vulture would just take her away on its wings. To her surprise, the vulture acquiesced, offering to take her to the grand mansion of the vulture chief. The chief, the vulture said, had known of the beautiful woman for some time and wanted her to become his queen. Her tears having ceased, the moon climbed up onto the bird's broad wings and flew with him through the sky to this new place.

As they approached their destination, the vulture pointed out a building that gleamed white in the distance. The vulture told her that it was the chief's home and was made of polished stone, though in fact it was only constructed with guano. When they arrived, the master of the shining mansion received the moon warmly. He embraced her, praising her beauty and promising to marry her. Thus, the moon became the lover of the chief. By some accounts, he was a majestic king vulture; by others, he was a four-eyed and four-horned devil.

Meanwhile, the sun and his brother both became worried when the moon did not return from gathering water. Together, they went down to the river. They saw the abandoned water jar on the bank, but did not find any sign of the moon. Immediately, the sun's brother regretted how severely he had spoken to his beloved.

The sun was pleased at his success in driving apart the two adulterers, but was angry that his wife was missing. He blamed his brother for her disappearance and ordered him to go look for her. The brother began to sob, because he did not know what had become of his lover, even when he ascended into the sky to look for her.

The sun did not want to compete with his brother for the moon's affections. He also realized that he could not kill his sibling. He decided to send him deep into the earth in the hope that he would not return. To trick his brother into descending, the sun convinced him that they should play a game that required jumping thrice on top of a board. After the sun completed his turn, his brother walked onto the board and sprung twice. When he landed the third time, the board broke in half and fell, along with the sun's brother, into a deep ravine.

Once he was alone, the sun began searching the riverbank for his wife. However, he did not find out what had happened to the moon until a blowfly buzzing past said that a vulture had borne away the radiant lady. It would not be easy to get ahold of the vulture, the blowfly advised, because the sun would have to trick him into coming down to earth.

After hearing this news, the sun set out to find a deer that would be willing to lend him its skin. Once he had borrowed the skin, he carried it back to the river from which his wife had intended to fetch water. The sun lay down on the bank and threw the deerskin over his body, covering himself so that he looked like a dead animal. Some say that he summoned the blowfly again and asked it to lay its eggs on the skin, as if it were a fresh carcass. Others claim that the sun merely requested that the insect rub salt into the skin. In both accounts, the sun also asked the blowfly to approach the flock of vultures circling in the sky above and bring the smell of carrion to them.

The blowfly obliged. As soon as the vultures caught the whiff of rotting deer, they called to the blowfly to ask about the source of the enticing smell. The insect told the scavengers that there was a deer carcass near the river below, and zoomed away as the vultures alighted next to the limp body. The last vulture to land on the riverbank was the same one who had brought the moon to their leader. Once the entire flock had landed, the scavengers moved in on the dead deer to plunge their beaks into the putrid feast.

This ceramic model, one of 23 figurines deposited in a seventh-century royal burial at El Peru-Waka', Petén, Guatemala, shows a man, perhaps a king, kneeling next to a deer. His closed eyes and crossed arms indicate that he is deceased, and the deer may be his *nawal* or companion spirit (see p. 205).

Peeking out from underneath the deerskin, the sun spotted the vulture who had carried away his wife. He sprang out and grabbed the bird's neck just as it was about to peck out his eye. The surprised vulture struggled to escape the sun's grip and began to choke. When the sun demanded to be taken to their chief, the vulture protested, "You are too heavy. I can't carry you!" The sun, however, was not fooled. "You carried the girl, so you can carry me," he said sternly. The vulture was forced to relent. After the sun clambered onto its strong, black wings, the pair took flight toward the chief's mansion.

Once the white house came into view, the sun ordered the vulture to drop him off on the ground below so that he could continue on foot. On the road, he came upon two men who were carrying a load of wood. He persuaded the walkers to let him hide amid the logs on their backs. Just as the men were about to enter town, he slipped out from the stacked wood and walked until he reached the chief's gleaming house.

When the sun arrived, he asked a servant if he could stay the night there. The servant replied that there was no room in the mansion, but he could stay in an empty hut nearby. Guided by the servant, the sun headed to the little shelter. Upon entering, he discovered two musical instruments, a long flute and a drum, stashed in the rafters. He also noticed seven (or, others say, fifteen) stray kernels of red maize scattered on the floor. Gathering the grains in his hands, he bored a small hole into each. After tossing the handful of kernels in the direction of the chief's house, he retrieved the flute and drum and began to make music in the hut as he waited for his plan to unfold.

Around the same time, the lord of the vultures began to feel severe pain in his teeth. Although he did not realize it, this was no ordinary toothache; it had been caused by the perforated red maize

Los Músicos (The Musicians), 1964, by Juan Sisay, a Tz'utujil painter from Santiago Atitlán, Sololá, Guatemala.

kernels that the sun had thrown towards his residence. The chief summoned all the local healers to treat him, but none could relieve his discomfort. As the pain worsened, the desperate chief ordered his servant to go to the newcomer in the hut and ask if he could cure the toothache. Under no circumstances, however, would the stranger be allowed into the lord's quarters.

The servant found the visitor playing the instruments and relayed his master's message. The sun rebuffed him, pointing out that there was no use in going to see what was wrong with the patient if he was not allowed to even look in his mouth. The servant returned

A Late Classic incense burner excavated from a noble residence at Palenque embodies an underworld jaguar god wearing a warrior headdress with symbolism associated with the Early Classic metropolis of Teotihuacan in central Mexico.

to the vulture lord, and the sun resumed making music. The same sequence of events repeated itself awhile later, with the servant arriving to communicate the chief's request for aid and the sun refusing because he was not allowed to approach his ailing host.

As the chief's pain continued to worsen, desperation overtook whatever suspicions he had toward the outsider. He summoned the servant and ordered him to go fetch the stranger again. This time, he promised that the visitor would be allowed to enter the chief's residence. The sun accepted the request and followed the servant back to the master's house.

When he entered the privileged space, he found the moon there, providing companionship to her new lover. In short order, the sun cured the toothache that he himself had caused. Relieved of his pain, the exhausted chief fell into a slumber. Once the vulture chief was asleep, the sun petitioned his wife to return with him. According to some accounts, the moon initially did not want to leave her new companion and had to be convinced to change her mind. Others contend that the moon was deeply unhappy with her new life and longed to escape back home.

In both versions, the moon eventually agreed to go back to her husband. The couple snuck out of the guano mansion, corralled two vultures, and rode on their wings back to the riverbank where they had begun their journey separately. Thus, the partnership between the sun and the moon was restored. When it became time for each to ascend into the sky to assume their celestial responsibilities, the sun took up the task of providing bright light to the earth during the day, and his wife served as the moon.

What happened to the sun's brother is more disputed. In the story from San Antonio, he is said to have risen into the sky, too, where he transformed into Venus as the morning star. According to the version from Senahú, however, he became clouds that ascend from valleys and canyons into the sky every morning. Thus, the drops that fall to earth as rain are tears that the brother continues to shed for his lost companion, the moon.

Coming Down to Earth

As with all Maya myths, the Tseltal and Q'eqchi' narratives about the origins of the sun and the moon reflect a combination of concepts inherited from ancient times and more recent innovations. The Maya have long conceptualized the moon and the sun as a cosmological duo and associated them with other complementary pairings. Even among the Classic Maya, the moon was consistently represented as female and the sun as male. A similar duality permeates the Tseltal and Q'eqchi' accounts of the relationship between the sun and the moon, even if the generational relationship between the two planetary bodies differs across mythological contexts.

Another facet of complementarity in the myths about solar and lunar origins is internecine rivalry. In both accounts, the brothers represent possible or alternative suns. Ultimately, the younger one triumphs to take his place in the sky at the expense of his older sibling. The young Tseltal protagonist, like his Chol and Tsotsil counterparts, orchestrates his brother's death and resurrection in animal form as revenge for a lifetime of abuse. In the Q'eqchi' tale, the older brother threatens the sun morally rather than physically by committing adultery with the sun's wife, the moon. After his defeat, the older brother becomes a lesser celestial feature, either rainclouds or Venus as the morning star.

Even with their distinct and at times contradictory details, the Tseltal and Q'eqchi' myths share an emphasis on the sun and moon's ties to the eternal cycle of life, death, and renewal. In both cases, the murdered older brother returns to fulfill other roles on earth or in the heavens. The Tseltal sun even endures daily decapitations, returning to life again and again before he finally defeats his sibling. The dialogical relationship between destruction and rejuvenation—the one being the necessary precursor to the other—is also fundamental to Maya accounts of the heavens and the underworld, which are the focus of the next chapter.

3

HEAVENS AND UNDERWORLD

Alongside the sun, rain is perhaps the most crucial factor determining the success or failure of a harvest. When conducted effectively, rituals for pluvial deities can prompt the arrival of much-needed rains. Neglecting ritual responsibility to the rain gods, however, can trigger communal devastation. To navigate these challenges, the Maya have long relied on skilled ritual practitioners to mediate between the people and celestial gods to ensure a productive agricultural season and, with it, collective survival. The next myth contextualizes the central Maya concern with rain within the relations between the gods, ritual practitioners, and their community. As told among the Ch'orti' in the municipality of Jocotán, Chiquimula, Guatemala, during the mid-twentieth to early twenty-first centuries, the tale of Kumix accounts for the rainy season's meteorological violence and milpa agriculture's ritual underpinnings. It also demonstrates the existential threat that the deviant behavior of a few can pose to the well-being of the community as a whole.

KUMIX SUMMONS THE RAINS

Some time ago, an infant angel named Kumix ended up in a stream. There are competing explanations for how he came to be there. Some claim that he originated in the foam that collected around

A Maya-style, Late Classic mural at Cacaxtla, Tlaxcala, Mexico, hundreds of kilometers northwest of the Maya area, depicts God L facing a fruit-laden cacao tree as his merchant's pack sits behind him. Behind the tree, a frog or toad crawls past a maize stalk bearing cobs shaped like the Maize god's head.

the opening of a watery vortex; others insist that he was born to a mother who abandoned him there, perhaps after attempting to abort the child. In yet another version, the boy was washing a wound on his shin when his vengeful older brothers attacked him and threw his bloodied remains into the water. All accounts agree, however, that the life of poor Kumix did not end in that stream.

Somehow, Kumix managed to pull himself out of the water and onto the bank, where he collapsed in exhaustion and tears. As it happened, an old lady was bathing or doing her washing nearby and heard the sobbing, which she followed to its distraught source. She had no children and had wanted a child of her own, so she was glad to take in the orphaned angel. After bundling Kumix in cloths, the aged woman brought the small boy home to raise as her own.

Hunters, two carrying deer carcasses and the other six blowing conch-shell trumpets, line up on a Classic Maya vessel.

The adoptive mother was no ordinary woman, but what the Ch'orti' refer to as a *k'ech'uj* or *sisimite*. Lanky, hairy, and capable of transitioning back and forth between human and animal form, these sinister creatures walk upright on backward feet and seek refuge in and around the cascades and streams that are their dominion. The Ch'orti' harbor a healthy fear of k'ech'uj. Known for their ravenous hunger, the beings survive by stealing food or kidnapping and eating humans, particularly children or travelers. As fate would have it, Kumix had ended up in this k'ech'uj's stream, so it was no coincidence that she had found him there. The boy's salvation from waters under the k'ech'uj's dominion marked him as exceptionally powerful, even godly, because no ordinary human would have survived.

Kumix's childhood was by no means carefree. His caretaker initially fed him with milk from her own breast. After the boy was weaned, however, he was constantly hungry because the k'ech'uj hoarded all their food for herself. By the time he reached adolescence, Kumix had become a skilled blowgunner who was able to fell the most elusive prey, even those which no other hunter could catch. He brought home so many birds that there were soon none left flying in the sky, so he had to begin hunting larger animals.

Yet the fruits of Kumix's labor were never enough to satisfy his adoptive mother.

Each night while he was sleeping, the k'ech'uj ate up everything that Kumix had brought home that day, leaving nothing left over. The boy rose each morning, empty stomach rumbling, and asked for food. The old woman scolded him, saying that he had eaten a full meal the night before and needed to go hunting again. If he did not bring back food for her that evening, she threatened, he would be her meal instead. Thus, the days passed. Kumix brought home an abundance of birds, tapirs, deer, and other game, but it was never enough to please his mother or to fill his own belly.

One day, when Kumix was out hunting, a bird—either a parrot or a dove, depending on the storyteller—spoke to him. He told the surprised angel that, unlike he had been raised to believe, the k'ech'uj was not his mother. His real mother was an angel residing

A Late Classic stucco portrait of an elderly woman from the Casa del Coral (Coral House) at El Mirador, Petén, Guatemala.

in the heavens. The k'ech'uj's partner, a giant, was not his father, either. Adding insult to injury, the bird delivered a second piece of shocking news: the reason that Kumix was always hungry was that the k'ech'uj and her partner had been eating all the game that he brought home. Incensed, Kumix refused to hunt or bring home food from that day forward.

This radical turn of events was unacceptable to the k'ech'uj. She had grown accustomed to her adoptive son providing for her insatiable needs. She began sharpening her teeth on a large rock, planning to eat Kumix instead. Before she could act, however, the boy took his own revenge. He swaddled a grinding stone in cloth and placed it in the hammock where he usually slept. The k'ech'uj approached and seized what she thought was the slumbering youth. She broke her teeth as she bit into the decoy, crying out in pain as blood spilled from her mouth.

After watching from the roofbeams as his adoptive mother tried to eat him, Kumix left the k'ech'uj for good. Some claim that he ran away under the pretense of fetching a remedy for the toothache that she had suffered from biting the stone. Others say that Kumix killed her before departing by burning her alive in their house. In other versions, the angel lured his adoptive mother into a milpa and set fire to it, leaving her to turn into a giant white stone in the barren field. Still other versions describe the boy shooting the k'ech'uj with his blowgun.

The adoptive mother's lover or partner—who may have been a giant, a tapir, or a fellow k'ech'uj—met a similar fate. In versions where the lover is a giant or male k'ech'uj, Kumix is said to have shot him with his blowgun. Those who say that the companion was a tapir recount how the angel trapped and castrated the beast and tricked his adoptive mother into eating its meat before killing

Maya Teeth

Tooth pain or damage is a recurring theme in Maya myths. Teeth are crucial to survival, as persons without them may be severely restricted in their nutrition, verbal communication, and oral health. The frequent reference to teeth in Maya storytelling likely reflects deeper cultural significance attached to the face, however. From the Classic period through modern times, Maya peoples have long emphasized the head and especially the face as the locus of individual identity and the self. Through Postclassic times, the Maya sometimes modified children's or adolescents' teeth by cutting notches into the sides (often producing a T-shaped sign that denoted "wind" or "breath"), filing the tip into a point, or drilling holes on the front for stone inlays. The procedures were painful and, if done poorly, could cause life-threatening infections. But they were important events in defining a Maya person in the transition to adulthood and in situating one's self in relation to the gods, whom the ancient Maya often portrayed with their own set of modified teeth. Damage to or loss of a tooth, in contrast, threatened not only one's health but one's identity—a fitting punishment, perhaps, for the k'ech'uj who tried to eat Kumix.

her, too. In any case, after destroying the k'ech'uj who had raised him and her partner, in a feat that no ordinary human could have accomplished, Kumix set off in search of his real mother.

Despite his extraordinary capabilities, Kumix could not reach the heavens alone. He asked a hawk to carry him skyward. Although the majestic predator agreed, it failed to take flight with the boy on its back. He next sought out a black vulture, which tried to lift up the youth with a tumpline wrapped around its forehead. The tumpline fell off in the air, however, and the pair came crashing back down to earth. The episode left the vulture with a raw, red forehead where the tumpline had sheared off its feathers, a feature still visible on the vulture today. Despite its best effort, a dove was similarly unable to help the increasingly desperate Kumix.

Discouraged by these setbacks, Kumix approached a modest hummingbird. The small creature was skeptical about its ability to fulfill the request, but agreed to give it a go. To lighten the hummingbird's load, Kumix shrunk himself to miniature form and stowed away in a guitar that dangled from the hummingbird's elegant neck. Thus, the courageous courier successfully bore its passenger up to heaven. Upon arriving, a grateful Kumix thanked the tiny bird by gifting it his blowgun, which it has worn ever since as its long, narrow bill.

Once in heaven, Kumix found his family—a family that, until recently, the orphan had never imagined having. It was not an entirely happy reunion, however. He learned that his father was long dead, and discovered his mother impoverished and naked, squatting in a run-down house with hardly anything to eat or drink. Her and her deceased husband's possessions, like those of all other inhabitants of the heavens, had been seized by the gang led by an impenetrable Bronze King, who had killed his father years earlier.

After hearing his mother's story, Kumix sent her out to get water for him to drink. While she was gone, he lit a piece of copal (pine resin) in his father's incense burner and censed the areas of the house where she stored beans, chicken, and maize with fragrant smoke. When his mother returned with the water, she found the bean and corn cribs brimming with food, and a whole flock of chickens squawking noisily. Overjoyed, she prepared atole and tortillas to eat together with her long-lost son. After the meal, Kumix set off into the forest to recover his parents' stolen possessions and to avenge his father's death.

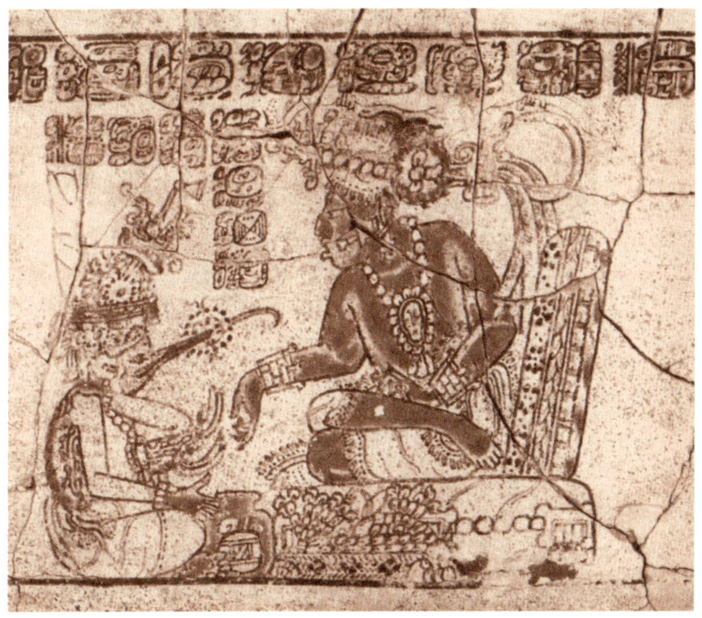

An anthropomorphic hummingbird sits with a jar of atole (maize gruel) before the throne of God D in this scene painted on a vessel excavated from a Late Classic tomb at Tikal, Petén, Guatemala.

First, Kumix had to confront the powerful Bronze King's compatriots, who were holding onto his father's belongings. The first was a howler monkey. Kumix persuaded it to drop his father's whip by offering it a bunch of ripe bananas. The second was a group of spider monkeys. They were holding his father's drum, which they beat to warn the reclusive Bronze King about approaching strangers. Kumix tricked the spindly simians into relinquishing the drum by offering to fill it with *pozol*. When the greedy monkeys hung the drum face-down from a tree to receive the warm maize drink, Kumix snatched the instrument and ran away before they could catch him.

A Classic Maya pendant in the shape of an armadillo, excavated from a deposit at Yaxha, Petén, Guatemala.

Next, Kumix sought out the armadillo who had become keeper of his father's seven coats. Using his father's whip, he forced the armored mammal out of its den. Once the armadillo had emerged, the youth may have continued to whip the armadillo until it handed over the clothing. In another version, Kumix covered himself with sawdust and said that it was lice, begging the armadillo to help him remove the bugs. The armadillo agreed and stripped off the coats in preparation, but before it could help the stranger, Kumix hit it with seven deadly bolts of lightning. Both versions explain why armadillos have a peculiar striped pattern on their backs even today; it is the scars left by Kumix's whipping or lightning strikes.

Kumix moved on to reclaim his father's sword, which a crocodile was vigilantly guarding in its mouth. To entice the reptile onto land, Kumix brought along a giant fish, or a bunch of bananas. Once the reptile had emerged from the water, Kumix conked it on the head with the help of a friendly rabbit. Yet the crocodile still would not open its mouth and drop the sword. Kumix and the rabbit took a more direct tack, and simply asked the creature where its vital center was located. For whatever reason, the crocodile confessed that it was at the base of its tail. Kumix and the rabbit immediately went over and struck that very spot, which prompted the crocodile to drop the sword as it curled into a ball.

The last piece for Kumix to recover was his father's ring. A giant wore the ornament in its mouth, where it was draped around a massive tooth. This time, Kumix received help from a rat, which he sent into the giant's lair as it slept. The rat tickled the nose of the slumbering giant, which let out a forceful sneeze that blew the ring out of its mouth. With the whip, drum, coats, sword, and ring in hand, Kumix hurried back home.

A Classic-period brick with a modeled crocodile from Comalcalco, Tabasco, Mexico.

After returning his father's long-lost belongings to his mother, Kumix was determined to return to the forest to defeat the Bronze King himself. His mother tried to deter him, warning that no angel could kill the fearsome being, who was protected by seven layers of bronze clothing. Even the behemoth's head was covered by seven bronze hats, and seven bronze sandals concealed his feet. But Kumix was not daunted. He had already devised a plot, based on his experience of fighting the Bronze King's animal associates.

Back in the forest, Kumix set about executing his plan. The angel found some sort of dirt or powder; some say he made it by crushing rotten logs, while others describe it as loose soil that he scooped up from the earth. In any case, Kumix enlisted a sympathetic swallow to take flight with a load of the dust on its back. He instructed the bird to fly above the unsuspecting Bronze King, flapping its wings to spill the dust along the nape of the King's neck and down its back.

As soon as the dust had fallen, the Bronze King found himself covered in large ants, either because the particles of dirt transformed into ants, or because the ants swarmed toward the smell of the rotten wood. As the crawling insects got under his armor and bit him fearlessly, he stripped off his bronze clothes. Desperate to rid himself of the ants, he removed all seven layers of the formidable armor. A waiting Kumix used his father's recovered sword to send a lightning bolt that struck the Bronze King dead on the spot.

Having avenged his father's death, Kumix returned home to his mother again. He went out to the family milpa, which had long been lying fallow. He summoned thunder by beating his father's drum and lightning by thrusting his father's sword; thus, Kumix called forth the rains needed to sustain the milpa's crops until harvest. It is for this reason that the Ch'orti' today count Kumix among their principal rain deities and describe the violent storms that often blow up during the rainy season as "Kumix's work."

What of the older brothers who had tried to kill the infant Kumix and left him stranded in the k'ech'uj's stream? Upon arriving in heaven, the angel discovered that his brothers were still back on earth, and had become immersed in an attempt to build a mountain so tall that they could reach the skies, where they would be reunited

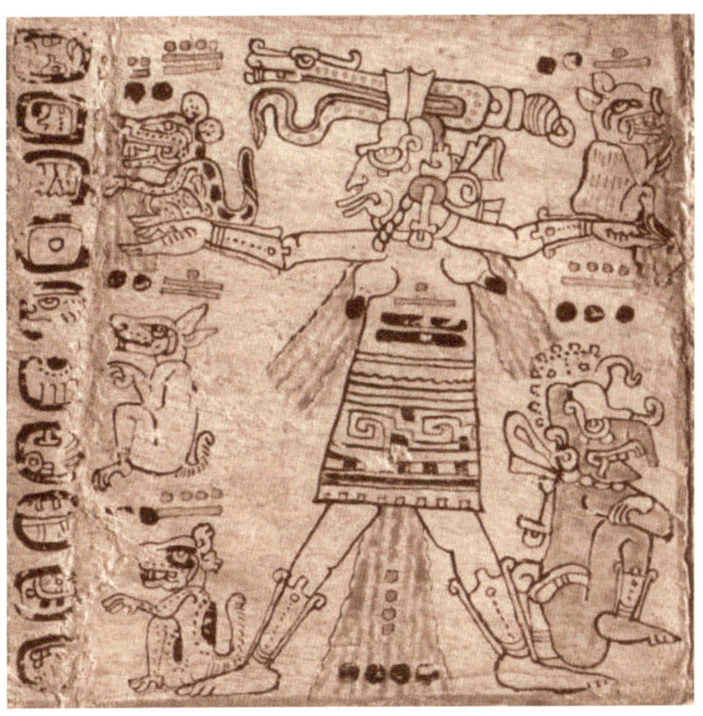

A Postclassic Yucatec illustration of water pouring from the body of creator goddess Chak Chel. Madrid Codex (fol. 30b).

with their mother. When Kumix told their mother the news, she was horrified, because she knew that if her elder sons managed to build such a bridge, massive eagles would descend from the heavens and ravage earth, including all the people living there. Kumix resolved to return to earth to pay his brothers a visit and convince them to halt the lethal project.

To help Kumix return to earth, his mother tied a string around him. Before slowly lowering him down from the skies, she gave her youngest son a little container of milk from her breast to show his brothers as proof that their mother had sent him. As she was letting Kumix down, however, the string broke just before he touched the ground. The youth fell the rest of the way to earth, scraping his knees and spilling some of the precious milk.

Kumix found his brothers, who were startled to see their youngest sibling alive after believing for so many years that he was dead. He told them that the construction posed a grave danger because of the fearsome eagles and other heavenly beasts who would descend to wipe out life on earth. After some persuading, they agreed to stop work, but told Kumix that he would have to destroy the unfinished mountain, because they could not do it themselves.

The youthful angel agreed and instructed his brothers to excavate small holes in the ground around the base of the mountain. Once the holes were ready, Kumix blindfolded his brothers and told them to position themselves head-first in the cavities, with their feet sprouting upward, to protect their eyes and faces from Kumix's work. Kumix called up a torrential rainstorm. Dark clouds appeared in the skies, and a deluge of rain suddenly poured down upon the brothers. As thunder roared, thick bolts of lightning descended from above, striking the mountain and leveling it back to earth.

The Storm god Chahk, brandishing an axe and an animated stone, confronts a frog or toad on a Late Classic ceramic vessel, from the central Maya lowlands.

During Kumix's work, four of his brothers broke their promise to keep their heads down and eyes shut. Because they snuck a glance to see how the mountain was destroyed, their vision was taken away from them, and they were permanently blinded. Some say that they were transformed into frogs, too, and that is why the croaking of frogs foreshadows impending rainfall.

After their transformation, the four disobedient brothers were ordered to occupy the mountains at the four corners of the world, where they were tasked with petitioning the arrival of the rains. It is to the four sightless angels, as representatives or associates of the powerful Kumix, that the Ch'orti' make a series of offerings or "payments" for the arrival and continuation of seasonal rains each year.

FROM THE SKIES TO THE UNDERWORLD

The Ch'orti' account of the angel named Kumix accounts for the annual recurrence of seasonal rains and rituals that accompany them. Its protagonist also embodies the archetypal Maya hero who protects the weak, rescues the struggling, and confronts the unjust. Generally, the Maya hero tends to be youthful and male. He is not physically weak, but he is not inordinately strong, either. What distinguishes him from his peers is cunning, the ability to identify weaknesses in his opponent, and to deceive them into making a mistake that can then be exploited to their detriment. It is his cleverness that allows the Maya hero to challenge antagonistic forces and, in many cases, to overcome unfavorable odds against an ostensibly more powerful opponent.

The most famous of all Maya heroes today are the brothers Junajpu' and Xb'alanke', whom we first met in Chapter 1. Among the Hero Twins' many adventures recorded in the *Popol Vuh*, their descent into the underworld, Xib'alb'a', and confrontation with its ruling lords is the best-known. The tale represents another variation on the theme of earthly forces triumphing over the dark underworld that we saw in the Classic Maya story about the clever rabbit (see pp. 47–56). Unlike that myth, however, the Hero Twins' exploits in Xib'alb'a' clearly illustrate how actions undertaken by a Maya hero—or, in this case, pair of heroes—are often predicated on their predecessors' setbacks. Just as Kumix had to restore his mother's inheritance and avenge his father's murder before he could save the world from celestial invasion, the Hero Twins must confront a series of challenges, including their own family's troubled legacy, before they can redefine the problematic relationship between the earth and the underworld.

The Hero Twins Triumph Over Xib'alb'a'

Long ago, according to the *Popol Vuh*, when the first ancestors walked the earth, the primordial couple Xpiyakok and Xmukane' had two sons, Jun Junajpu' and Wuqub' Junajpu'. They were avid ballplayers who spent much of their free time playing on the ballcourt. But their heavy footfall and shouts disturbed Jun Kame' and Wuqub' Kame', lords of Xib'alb'a'. Irritated by the ruckus, the aptly yclept pair—their names mean "One Death" and "Seven Death," respectively—convened their underworld companions. The noxious bunch collectively represented all the decay, bodily fluids, and death of the world above. They agreed on a plan to lure the brothers into Xib'alb'a' to steal their fine ballplaying gear. Once the boys had been extinguished, the underworld lords' peace could finally be restored.

One day, four owls landed at the ballcourt where Jun Junajpu' and Wuqub' Junajpu' were immersed in a ballgame. The grisly messengers told the boys that Jun Kame' and Wuqub' Kame' wanted to invite them down for a competition, and that they should bring their ballgame equipment. Unaware of the true motive behind the invitation, Jun Junajpu' and Wuqub' Junajpu' agreed to visit the underworld to play against the lords. Immediately, they went home to inform their mother. After securing their rubber ball in the rafters of the house for safekeeping, the brothers assured their weeping mother that they would return safely to her and to Jun Junajpu's two sons who lived with them, Jun B'atz' and Jun Chowen.

The messengers flew ahead to guide the brothers' descent into Xib'alb'a'. The path was rugged, taking Jun Junajpu' and Wuqub' Junajpu' across deep canyons and roaring rivers flowing with scorpions, blood, and pus. After some time, they reached a junction of

Classic Maya Ballgame

Like all major Indigenous Mesoamerican civilizations, the pre-colonial Maya played a ballgame (*pitz* in Classic Mayan) whose function appears to have mixed ritual, politics, entertainment, and sport. At least one ballcourt, minimally consisting of a central corridor flanked on either long side by low, parallel stone buildings, can be found at almost every major archaeological site. Many Classic Maya kings proudly identified themselves as ballplayers (*aj-pitz*), and the game was a common subject of text and imagery. The ball was made of rubber and varied in size; some Classic Maya texts indicate that a ball's circumference could exceed 3 m (10 ft). No record survives of how the game was played, but surviving pictures and comparisons with other Mesoamerican traditions offer some clues.

A common Classic Maya variant of the game seems to have required players—most of whom are illustrated as men competing in two opposing teams or, occasionally, as dueling individuals—to use their bodies to bounce the ball up and down the narrow corridor or playing field. The main restriction seems to have been that they could not use their hands, feet, or head. To protect their hips and generate more force against the ball, ballplayers wore large rings of padding, or yokes, around their midsections, as well as protective guards on their knees or shins. The goal was apparently to maneuver the ball into a zone at the opponents' end of the ballcourt. Some ballcourts have rings affixed to the stone walls through which players hit the ball to score, but these devices did not become widespread until the Postclassic period.

four roads, each a different color. They turned onto the black one, leaving the red, white, and yellow paths behind.

Seeing the shadowy outlines of figures along the black road and thinking that they were their divine hosts, Jun Junajpu' and Wuqub'

The Maya strongly associated the ballgame with the underworld, death, and sacrifice. This connection is represented in the *Popol Vuh*'s account of the Hero Twins' exploits in Xib'alb'a', and is amply attested archaeologically in the form of weapons and remains of human sacrifice that have been excavated at Maya ballcourts. Classic and Postclassic Maya imagery makes this connection explicit as well, with some scenes depicting sacrificial victims or skulls inside the bouncing ball. Although the ballgame was surely played for fun and entertainment on some occasions, competition could also ritually transform a ballcourt into the arena for a cosmological battle between the forces of life and death.

Sculpted panel from La Corona, Petén, Guatemala, depicting two Late Classic Maya ballplayers squaring off with a large ball between them.

Junajpu' greeted them as Jun Kame' and Wuqub' Kame'. The lords of Xib'alb'a' broke out into raucous laughter when they heard this. They knew then that they had deceived the brothers, for the figures were not the lords but merely effigies carved from wood.

Color-Directional Symbolism

The structure of the Maya cosmos is usually characterized as quadripartite and defined by four corners. Depending on the tradition, the corners are usually associated either with the four cardinal directions (north, south, east, west) or the four major points on the sun's path (sunrise, zenith, sunset, nadir). At the middle of the cosmos is the World Tree that stretches up toward the sky above (see Chapter 1).

Like many Indigenous peoples in the Americas, the Maya have long associated the cosmos's four corners and center with colors. Typically, north or zenith is linked with white, east or sunrise with red, south or nadir with yellow, west or sunset with black, and the center with blue-green. These associations have remained quite stable over the course of Maya history and are attested as early as the Classic period in inscriptions that record hieroglyphs for the colors alongside the (still undeciphered) hieroglyphs for the directions. Thus, the black path leads Jun Junajpu' and Wuqub' Junajpu down into the underworld, where the sun descends after its daily journey across the sky.

When the brothers arrived in the realm of the underworld lords, Jun Kame' and Wuqub' Kame' offered them a bench on which to take a seat and rest from their long journey. Unsuspecting, they sat down, only to be severely burned by the hot stone. Their surprise and pain just elicited more laughter from the onlookers. Once again, the lords had tricked the twins.

The hosts showed the guests to the house where they would spend the night, promising to bring a torch and cigars because it was so cold and dark inside. But when the lords of Xib'alb'a' returned with the burning torch and lit cigars, they ordered Jun Junajpu' and Wuqub' Junajpu' to return them the next morning unused.

Late nineteenth-century Yucatec men descend into a deep cenote or underground cave to fill ceramic jars with water to carry back up to the surface.

In the end, the brothers never had a chance to play the ballgame with their hosts. By the next morning, the torch and cigars had burned out. Seeing that Jun Junajpu' and Wuqub' Junajpu' had failed the overnight trial, the Xib'alb'a' lords sacrificed and buried them in the underworld ballcourt.

Before interring the bodies, the underworld gods decapitated Jun Junajpu' and hung his head in a calabash tree near the road. The tree had been barren, but with Jun Junajpu's head amid its branches, it began to bear fruit in the likeness of the severed head. Observing the tree's transformation, the lords forbade anyone from going near it or harvesting calabashes from its branches.

But not even the strictest prohibition could keep the underworld inhabitants away from the enchanted tree forever. The daughter of one of the Xib'alb'a' lords—whose name, Ixkik' ("Lady Blood"),

Late Preclassic mural from San Bartolo, Petén, Guatemala, showing the Principal Bird Deity perched atop a World Tree laden with ripe calabashes.

Detail from a Late Classic vessel showing the Maize god's head growing from a cacao tree.

reflects her distasteful origins—approached the peculiar tree one day after her father told a story that sparked her curiosity. As she admired the branches laden with strangely shaped calabashes, she sighed enviously and wondered aloud if any harm would actually come to her if she picked the fruit.

Suddenly, Jun Junajpu's skull spoke out in response from among the branches, where it hung indistinguishable from the other calabashes in the tree. The unfamiliar voice inquired whether Ixkik' truly desired the tree's fruit. She insisted that she did, and the voice instructed her to stretch out her right hand. Jun Junajpu's skull spit into Ixkik's open palm, impregnating her. He assured the maiden that she would not die. Instead, she should ascend to the earth's surface, where she would bear offspring who would inherit their father's greatness.

Ixkik' returned to her underworld home and waited. As her belly grew, her father realized what had happened. Together with the other lords, he decided to send emissaries to sacrifice her and her unborn offspring. When they arrived, however, Ixkik' refused to submit to her father's wishes, recalling Jun Junajpu's promise that she would not die. She sent the underworld messengers back with a ball of red copal instead of her heart. Thus, she deceived her father, who believed that the sacrifice had been completed.

Ixkik' ascended to earth, where she sought out and found Jun Junajpu's mother, Xmukane'. Initially, the matriarch did not believe Ixkik's story. Xmukane' told the underworld maiden that she could prove herself by going to collect a large bundle of maize from a milpa that the old woman knew contained only one dry ear of maize. When Ixkik' nevertheless returned awhile later with a net brimming with maize, Xmukane' realized that her story was true, and finally received Ixkik' into the home that Jun Junajpu' and Wuqub' Junajpu' had once left behind. There, Ixkik' gave birth to twin boys, Junajpu' and Xb'alanke'—the Hero Twins.

Growing up, Junajpu' and Xb'alanke' were not Xmukane's favorite grandchildren. She preferred the boys' older half-brothers, Jun B'atz' and Jun Chowen, whose mother had passed away even before their father, Jun Junajpu', had descended into Xib'alb'a'.

One day, when they were working in the milpa, the Hero Twins caught a rat. They were about to kill it when the rat began speaking to them. It revealed that their father and uncle had died in Xib'alb'a', and had hidden their ballgame equipment in the rafters of their mother's house before descending into the underworld. Later, the rat helped the brothers retrieve the gear and hide it near the ballcourt, where they began to play.

The lords of Xib'alb'a' had been enjoying the tranquility that had been restored to the underworld since the demise of Jun Junajpu' and Wuqub' Junajpu'. Thus, they were surprised to hear the aboveground stomping resume. Incensed, they sent messengers up to the earth's surface to find the source of the din and bring the perpetrators down to the underworld. The emissaries went to the home of Xmukane' and told her that Jun Kame' and Wuqub' Kame', lords of the underworld, had summoned her youngest grandsons to appear before them within seven days. The aged woman wept despairingly, recalling how her sons had received a similar invitation and had never returned from Xib'alb'a'.

Childbirth, 2010, by Julian Coche Mendoza, a Tz'utujil painter from San Juan La Laguna, Sololá, Guatemala.

Xmukane' sent a louse to find Junajpu' and Xb'alanke' and bring them home. On the road, the louse met a toad, who offered to transport the louse in his belly so he could arrive sooner to the ballcourt. The louse agreed. The toad promptly ate the louse, but did not travel much faster than the insect had. A snake came and, upon learning that the toad was carrying a messenger, made a similar offer to swallow him and speed up his journey. The toad accepted. The snake was soon gulped down by a falcon, who finally arrived at the ballcourt where the twins were contentedly playing the ballgame.

Startled by the sudden appearance of the visitor, Junajpu' and Xb'alanke' shot down the falcon with their blowgun, hitting the bird in the eye. The falcon told the boys that he had a message for them that he would share after they had cured his eye. After the twins replaced the damaged eye with their rubber ball, the falcon vomited the snake, who vomited the toad, who tried to vomit the louse but just slobbered. The boys wrenched open the toad's mouth and found the louse clinging to its teeth. Finally, the louse spoke: Junajpu' and Xb'alanke' were to return home to their grandmother, who was grieving because they had been summoned by Jun Kame' and Wuqub' Kame' to play ball in Xib'alb'a'.

Back at home, the twins tried to comfort Xmukane'. Just as their father and uncle had done, they assured the matriarch that they would return safely. As a sign of their promise, each boy planted an ear of young, unripe maize in the dry earth at the center of the house. If it shrivels, they told her, we have died; but if it sprouts green and grows, you will know that we are alive. Junajpu' and Xb'alanke' gathered their blowguns and set off for the underworld, across the same rugged landscape that their father and uncle had traversed years before.

This shell-and-jade mosaic of a skeletal death god was among a wealth of offerings buried alongside a Late Classic nobleperson at Topoxte, Petén, Guatemala.

Over the rivers of scorpions, blood, and pus, they followed the messenger-guides to the colored crossroads, where they turned onto the black road to Xib'alb'a'. The twins, however, were shrewder than their father and uncle had been. Before continuing down the black road, Junajpu' plucked a hair from his knee. He asked it to fly ahead and poke the figures lining the dimly lit path ahead as if it were a mosquito.

First, the hair-mosquito encountered two wooden effigies, which did not react to the prick. But the next twelve figures each cried out in pain when they felt what seemed like a mosquito bite. In their surprise, they called out to each other by name. Thus, the twins knew to ignore the two figures at the front of the line, which were just wooden carvings. They could also greet Jun Kame', Wuqub' Kame', and their ten noxious companions by name as they passed down the road, having heard the figures react to the hair-mosquito's jab.

When they arrived at the end of the row, Jun Kame' and Wuqub' Kame' met the visitors and invited them to take a seat on the nearby bench to rest. Unlike their father and uncle, the twins refused. They knew that the stone was hot and would burn them. Frustrated that they had yet to deceive the boys, the Xib'alb'a' lords sent Junajpu' and Xb'alanke' to the first trial.

Just like Jun Junajpu' and Wuqub' Junajpu', the twins spent the first night in the underworld in a cold, dark house, where they received a burning torch and lit cigars and were told to return all three items unused in the morning. The twins put out the torch and cigars and fixed red macaw feathers to the ends of each. Thus, the custodians watching them overnight were deceived into thinking that the items were still alight. Jun Kame' and Wuqub' Kame' were astonished and even a bit shaken when they returned the next day to find the twins holding the unused torch and cigars.

The Xib'alb'a'ns challenged Junajpu' and Xb'alanke' to a ballgame and insisted on playing with their underworld ball. But theirs was no ordinary ball. It looked like a skull, and when the underworld lords threw it in front of Junajpu's yoke, a round, sharp blade laced with bones sprang out from it and rampaged around the ballcourt. Seeing this, Junajpu' and Xb'alanke' accused the underworld lords of trying to kill them and threatened to leave the game. The Xib'alb'a'ns relented and agreed to play with the boys' rubber ball—on the condition that, if they won, the boys would have to bring them flowers the next morning: one bowl each of red, white, yellow, and large petals.

The match was closely contested, but in the end, Junajpu' and Xb'alanke' were forced to concede. The denizens of the underworld rejoiced, knowing that the boys would not be able to gather the flower petals for them by morning. That same night, they sent the twins to their second trial, for which they had to sleep in a house filled with razor-sharp blades that threatened to cut them to death. But the boys ordered the blades to be still, and they did not move for the rest of the night. Meanwhile, Junajpu' and Xb'alanke' called ants to come to their aid. They asked the ants to gather flower petals from the underworld garden of Jun Kame' and Wuqub' Kame'. The ants slipped unnoticed past the watchmen whom the Xib'alb'a' lords had ordered to guard the garden overnight and brought piles of flowers back to the brothers.

Reconstructed view of the Late Classic Ballcourt A-III at Copan, Honduras, looking northward.

The next morning, Jun Kame' and Wuqub' Kame' were amazed to see that the twins had survived the night among the vicious blades. What's more, they had assembled the bowls of colored petals just as the underworld lords had ordered them to. The Xib'alb'a'ns played another ballgame against the visitors that day. This time, however, neither side was able to overcome the other. At the end of the day, the underworld lords sent Junajpu' and Xb'alanke' to spend the night in the frigid house filled with ice and cold winds. Instead of freezing to death, the twins survived. Much to the lords' chagrin, they returned in the morning to find the boys very much alive.

Thus, Junajpu' and Xb'alanke' progressed successfully through the remaining trials of Xib'alb'a'. In the house of jaguars, they fed bones to the hungry animals. The watchmen, hearing the predators gnawing, thought that the great felines were feasting on the boys' bodies. After the twins emerged alive from the house of jaguars, they were sent to the house filled with fire. They did not die there, either, emerging unharmed from the flames, although the *Popol Vuh* does not explain how. They spent the next night in the house of bats, where they crawled inside their blowguns to escape the vicious creatures' bites. There, however, the twins finally faltered.

Impatient for dawn to come so that they could leave the bat house, Xb'alanke' asked his brother if he could see day breaking. Junajpu' stuck his head out of the blowgun to take a look. At that precise moment, a bat swooped down and cut off the boy's head. When Junajpu' did not reply to his calls, Xb'alanke' realized that he was dead. The lords of Xib'alb'a' had finally defeated them. Overjoyed, Jun Kame' and Wuqub' Kame' displayed Junajpu's head at the ballcourt as a symbol of their victory. But Xb'alanke' would not give up so easily.

Early that same morning, Xb'alanke' called together all the animals, large and small. He asked each creature to bring him the food that they ate. Among the many foods brought back was a chilacayote squash, which a coati contributed. The creator gods carved it into a likeness of Junajpu's severed head. Once the squash was ready, Xb'alanke' summoned a rabbit. He told the leporid to lie in wait among the tomato plants that were growing near one end of the ballcourt. When a rubber ball rolled by, Xb'alanke' said, the rabbit should emerge from the plants and hop away as fast as possible.

When the morning light settled, a new ballgame began. This time, they played with Junajpu's head as the ball; Junajpu's body wore only the chilacayote squash. The underworld lords threw down Junajpu's head to begin play, and Xb'alanke' used his yoke to hit it up over the ballcourt. After bouncing twice, it landed squarely in the tomato patch, prompting the rabbit to dart out of its hiding place. Thinking that the rabbit was the ball, the lords of Xib'alb'a' gave chase.

Meanwhile, Xb'alanke' ran over to the tomato plants, retrieved Junajpu's head, and reunited it with the body, thus reviving his brother. The twins threw the carved chilacayote squash into the

A Late Classic Maya shell pendant in the shape of a rabbit, including its stub of a tail.

ballcourt and called to their opponents to come back, saying that they had found the ball. They resumed playing until the squash broke open. As seeds and fibrous flesh spilled onto the playing field, the underworld lords realized that they had been deceived.

Junajpu' and Xb'alanke' knew that Jun Kame' and Wuqub' Kame' had been plotting their deaths. After the game ended, the twins summoned two diviners and instructed them how they should respond when the Xib'alb'a' lords asked how to kill the boys for good. The wisemen were to tell the underworld rulers to roast the brothers in an oven, grind up their bones like flour, and scatter the bone dust into the underworld river. Thus, the twins had already prepared a plan when the underworld messenger came a short time later to tell them that Jun Kame' and Wuqub' Kame' wanted to see them.

The Hero Twins arrived to find that the underworld lords had prepared a pit oven, which was already burning hot with fire. Junajpu' and Xb'alanke' entered the oven without protest, telling the lords that they knew that they would die. Delighted by their victory, the Xib'alb'a' lords called the two diviners to ask what they should do with the bones. Just as Junajpu' and Xb'alanke' had requested, the diviners told them to grind up the bones one by one and scatter the dust into the river, so that the flowing water would carry away the remains. Thus, the Hero Twins were reduced to powder and thrown into the underworld river. Yet the underworld lords' triumph would only be temporary.

Six days after the death of Junajpu' and Xb'alanke', two poor orphans appeared in Xib'alb'a'. Ugly and dressed in rags, they delighted the underworld denizens with many dances. They also performed magic tricks. First, they burned down a house and instantly rebuilt it. From there, they demonstrated more daring feats. They even took

An Early Postclassic relief from Chichen Itza, Yucatán, Mexico, depicts a ballplayer (left) holding the head of his decapitated opponent (right).

turns sacrificing each other, only to come to life again. The Xib'alb'a'ns greatly enjoyed the entertainment. Jun Kame' and Wuqub' Kame' soon got wind of the performers and sent for them to demonstrate their abilities before them and their associates.

A crowd gathered to watch the spectacle. The urchins performed their dances, until the lords asked the orphans to sacrifice and revive their dog. After the orphans successfully carried out that feat, Jun Kame' asked them to burn down and rebuild his house. He was amazed that his house seemed untouched after the boys' stunt. The orphans performed a heart sacrifice on one Xib'alb'a'n and immediately restored his life. One of the boys even cut up the other and put him back together, good as new.

Entranced, Jun Kame' and Wuqub' Kame' entreated the orphans to sacrifice them, too. The orphans humbly agreed to perform the trick on their hosts. They excised the underworld lords' hearts, just as they had done to the other Xib'alb'a'n. But this time, they did not

Maya Sacrifice

Through the Postclassic period, Maya peoples performed a wide variety of sacrifices in order to provide sustenance to the gods and ancestors, reciprocating the well-being that they provided to humans. Non-human offerings ranged from incense and rubber to foodstuffs and animals, and were frequently burned to transform them into a medium accessible to their supernatural recipients. Today, ceremonies performed by highland Maya ritual specialists may include copal, alcohol, food, candles, and flowers, among other items. Prior to Spanish colonialism, human sacrifice was widely practiced as well. Some iterations, like letting blood from the mouth or genitals or removing fingers, would have been painful but not life-threatening. Heart sacrifice, in contrast, entailed extracting the vital organ of an often living captive or another subject by cutting open the chest through, under, or above the rib cage. The dramatic performance, which seems to have been the exclusive purview of elites, typically took place in public spaces before a crowd of onlookers and was as much a statement of worldly authority as a presentation to the gods.

revive their subjects. They left Jun Kame' and Wuqub' Kame' dead, terrifying the other Xib'alb'a'n gods. In that moment, the strange orphans revealed themselves to be Junajpu' and Xb'alanke'. They had returned from the dead to the underworld to avenge the deaths of their father and uncle. The remaining underworld lords realized that they had been defeated.

Terrified by the twins' powers, the lords of Xib'alb'a' wept and implored the twins to take pity on them. The twins agreed to spare their lives. But thenceforth, the underworld would no longer be nourished with human hearts and human blood, nor with pristine material gifts. The people on earth would sacrifice red copal and

In this scene on a Late Classic Maya vessel, a sacrificial victim lies prone on a stone altar as his torso is cut open by a masked figure's blade.

blood that already had been dirtied by falling on the ground. At the end of the year, they would only offer the underworld lords their old pots, to make way for new household goods for the coming year. Because of the Hero Twins' triumph, the lords of Xib'alb'a' would never reclaim the greatness that they had previously enjoyed.

After their victory, Junajpu' and Xb'alanke' retrieved their father's head from the calabash tree. They also retrieved Jun Junajpu' and Wuqub' Junajpu's bodies from the underworld ballcourt, leaving behind only Jun Junajpu's heart. The brothers ascended to the surface of the earth and returned to their grandmother, alive and triumphant.

Heroic Interdependence and Reciprocity

According to the *Popol Vuh*, Jun Junajpu's initial demise did not just precede his sons' triumph temporally. Junajpu' and Xb'alanke's victory over the lords of Xib'alb'a', which limited the underworld's power over earth and lightened humanity's sacrificial obligations to the lords of Xib'alb'a', would not have been possible without their father's death. Jun Junajpu's decapitated head impregnated their mother, an underworld maiden. As a result of the scandal, the twins were raised by their less-than-affectionate grandmother on earth. There, the boys learned about their father and uncle's hobby, found the hidden rubber ball, and began playing with it. Only then did they attract the attention of the underworld lords and receive the same invitation to Xib'alb'a' that had doomed their predecessors.

Family history positioned the twins to avenge the wrong done to their father and uncle. Yet what set them apart from their predecessors was a cleverness that allowed them to triumph over the lords of Xib'alb'a'. They watchfully anticipated the underworld rulers' deceptions; they also devised novel tricks to meet the lords' unreasonable demands. Eventually, the lords fell victim to their own scheming, allowing the younger, humbler, and apparently weaker protagonists to triumph. Perhaps just as importantly, the Hero Twins were willing to receive and solicit aid. They masterminded strategies, but did not overcome the trials of Xib'alb'a' alone. Relying on the strengths of allies, especially animals and other gods, allowed them to achieve feats beyond the reach of their personal capabilities.

The Hero Twins embody another basic feature of Maya heroes, namely that their status is not contingent on a successful outcome of individual efforts. Heroes sometimes fall short or lose a battle—or even their lives—to an opponent. In such cases, they are not ridiculed or

A stone altar that marked the center of the Late Classic ballcourt at Copan shows two heavily clad players facing each other across a large ball, labeled in hieroglyphs as a *k'an tuun* ("precious stone") or *k'ahn tuun* ("flat stone").

considered less worthy of respect for having made the attempt. Instead, heroic narratives often frame a fallen protagonist's shortcomings as a prelude for success achieved later, either by the same actor or by a successor. From this perspective, Maya heroism is defined as much by multigenerational inheritance as by individual behavior. The path to becoming a hero is neither easy nor straight, and a relay of protagonists may be required to reach the destination. A primordial template for Maya heroism can be found in the biography of another foundational character, the Maize god, whose story accounts for the inevitable cycle of birth, death, and renewal that sustains the Maya cosmos.

4

MILPA

The Maya have always known that they were not the first to inhabit the cosmos, nor would they be the last. Before them, the creators had forged other beings—plants, animals, other gods—to fill the world, some of which subsequently disappeared to make room for newcomers. Even after the first humans were shaped, scores of Maya ancestors had paved the way for their descendants to take on the work of caring for the gods, maintaining cultural traditions, and upholding social norms. For the Maya, there has traditionally been no clear distinction between what English speakers would call a "god" and an "ancestor." Many mythical protagonists combine mortal and supernatural traits, and are referred to using a combination of human kinship terms and epithets reserved for otherworldly beings. To what extent these predecessors were "human" like the narrators of their stories is largely irrelevant, in other words. What matters is the legacy that they established for the Maya who came after them.

Perhaps the most prominent early progenitor was the Maize god, who was arguably the most important deity among the Maya prior to the introduction of Catholicism in the sixteenth century. Scholars have reconstructed a Classic Maya account of the Maize god's biography based on imagery and hieroglyphic inscriptions and on comparison with similar narratives that have been recorded since colonial times. Like other divine beings, the Maize god was variable in physical form and could appear in numerous aspects. One of the

In this Postclassic portrait, the Maize god holds a plump, round tamale (*waaj*), which "he eats" (*u-mak'*), according to the accompanying hieroglyphic text. Dresden Codex (p. 13b).

An early eighth-century Late Classic sculpture of the Maize god from Copan, Honduras.

most common Classic-period manifestations was Juun Ixiim, who represented mature corn, with a tassel of silky hair affixed to his forehead. The other was Waxak Ajan, the embodiment of a young ear of corn whose head was marked with kernels.

Across his diverse appearances, the Maize god was consistently visualized as a youthful male, with his sloping forehead, silky hair, and handsome face representing the epitome of Maya beauty. Many infants, especially in noble families, had their heads shaped after the elegant, elongated form of the Maize god's cob-shaped crown. In their many dances, too, the Classic Maya mimicked the graceful steps and back-and-forth movement that had earned the deity the status of the mythic originator of dance.

Maize and Milpa

The Maize god's centrality among the Maya directly reflects the staple food's centrality in local diet and culture. First domesticated in southwestern Mexico nearly 9,000 years ago, maize has been cultivated in the Maya lowlands since at least 5,500 years ago. By about 4,000 years ago, the grain had become the basic staple in the Maya region, accounting for at least 70 percent of an individual's food intake.

Although maize in its pure form is not as nutritious as some other staple grains, such as sorghum, wheat, or millet, the ancient Indigenous process of nixtamalization, during which grains are soaked in limewater, enhances maize's nutritional quality by releasing niacin (vitamin B3). The limewater's softening effect also separates the hull from the kernel, making grinding easier for preparation of a variety of maize-based dishes. Among the Classic and Postclassic Maya, the basic form in which the foodstuff was consumed was the tamale, a dense, steamed cornbread (from Nahuatl *tamalli*). There is some evidence that tortillas, the elemental unit of maize consumption in central Mexico, were consumed by the Classic Maya, too. The flat, circular bread was not widely adopted across the region until the colonial period, however.

For some four millennia, maize has been the centerpiece of the local agricultural system known as the milpa. This intercropping system, in which beans, squash, chilis and other crops are cultivated among maize, is adapted to the naturally thin soil atop the region's bedrock. Traditionally, milpa agriculture entails a slash-and-burn rotation in which vegetation is burned to inject phosphorus, potassium, and other nutrients into the soil and to clear the area for planting before the onset of the rainy season. After a few harvests, the land lies fallow—ideally for several years—and the farmer rotates to another plot. Since the colonial period, however, Maya access to land has been dramatically reduced. As a result, milpa farmers have been forced to reduce or eliminate fallow periods, which has severely limited the agricultural system's efficacy.

Dried maize stalks in a milpa in Todos Santos Cuchumatán, Huehuetenango, Guatemala, January 1977.

AN ETERNAL CYCLE OF DEATH AND REBIRTH

For all the life-giving sustenance that the harvest brings to milpa farmers, its completion marks the end of life for the Maize god. Cob after cob is tugged from the stalk with a twist of the arm, literally and figuratively beheading the plant. Bare stalks, stripped of their ripe ears of corn, stand dry and barren in the milpa. In this way, the Maize god is sacrificed and summoned into the watery underworld at the end of every agricultural season.

The sources do not tell us how the Maize god receives the call from the underworld lords. But we do know that the youthful god does not make the journey alone. Accompanying him is a series of animal companions, including a spider monkey, a macaw, and an iguana. Like the Maize god himself, they raise their wrists to their faces in an expression of sorrow and dismay. A duo of aged deities, nicknamed the Paddler gods, guides the despondent party. We do not know their names, but their features are distinctive. One has the spots, ears, and nose of an underworld jaguar, and the septum of the other is pierced by a long stingray spine. Together, the old gods paddle the canoe that transports the dying Maize god and his cohort down into the underworld.

The Paddler gods ferry the Maize god (center) and his animal companions to the underworld. The scene was incised on a bone buried in the tomb of Late Classic king Jasaw Chan K'awiil I at Tikal, Petén, Guatemala.

Once in the underworld, the deceased Maize god is wrapped in cloth or reed mats and laid out on a bier. Mourners then assemble to pay their respects and express their lamentation. Display of the mortuary bundle and other rites around the Maize god's death take place deep within the mythical Sustenance Mountain, whose dark, moist interior is the primordial place of origin for maize and other crops. The yawning caves in Sustenance Mountain are also the resting place of privileged ancestors and gods. They are thus home to the full cycle of life and death. For this reason, Classic Maya kings embedded their own tombs in towering pyramids, which they commissioned as stone representations of the mythical location of the Maize god's funeral. In this way, kings physically and symbolically contextualized their death as a prelude to their rebirth as venerated ancestors, following the precedent set by the Maize god.

After the mourning period, the Maize god's funerary bundle is buried underground. As it decomposes back into the earth from which he was once born, other seeds sprout above his burial place. His remains become the fertile ground from which mythical, anthropomorphic trees take root and grow, bearing cacao, avocado, zapote, and other important foodstuffs. In death, the Maize god gives life to another generation of plants that will bear the next crop of seeds and fruits.

With each kernel of maize that a milpa farmer plants, the Maize god has a chance to grow anew. The deity's rejuvenation begins with rebirth from the jaws of a piscine serpent, yet another denizen of the aquatic underworld. The reborn Maize god is dressed by a cohort of women, who drape him in brilliant jade and *Spondylus* shell jewels, a beaded skirt, and an ornate headdress, even as their

Scenes incised on an Early Classic vase show the Maize god as a mortuary bundle lying on a bier (top) and as a skeleton above which new trees are sprouting (bottom).

own bodies remain unadorned. Only then is he ready to depart the underworld.

The Maize god leaves much as he arrived, in a canoe paddled by the pair of aged deities who had guided his descent. In some images of the scene, he clutches a large bundle, which may be filled with maize kernels to be planted above. In others, a turtle-shell drum or rattle accompanies the reborn deity, indicating that he ascends to the sound of music.

Still, the canoe journey alone is not enough for a seed to germinate. Just as nascent plant life must access the sun's rays to flourish, the Maize god must penetrate Sustenance Mountain to begin his lifecycle anew on the earth's surface. For this step, he relies on the aid of divine compatriots. Chahk, the Classic Maya Storm god, splits open the dry and cracked earth, his stone weapon thundering as

A ceramic vase shows the Maize god's rebirth in the watery underworld (bottom left), his adornment (left), and his ascent to earth in a canoe guided by the Paddler gods (top right).

he dances and strikes the ground. The Classic Maya Lightning god, K'awiil, also accompanies the Maize god's emergence.

In some Classic Maya renditions, two youthful gods, Juun Ajaw and Yax Baluun, also accompanied the Maize god's ascent to the earth's surface. Based on their names and physical attributes, the pair can be identified as Classic Maya versions of the Hero Twins known from the colonial K'iche' *Popol Vuh*, whom we learned about in Chapters 2 and 3. In the case of the Maize god's rebirth, however, the pair's contributions are unclear. Yax Baluun, whose body is marked with patches of jaguar pelt, holds a large jar and pours water into the dry earth from which the Maize god has just sprung. Juun Ajaw, for his part, sows the maize kernels that the reborn deity brought with him from the underworld.

Although individual Classic Maya versions of the Maize god's mythical biography varied, the message was the same: Without the stormy fanfare of the rainy season, the unending wheel of the Maize god's lifecycle would cease to turn. Reborn out of the watery underworld, the deity dances back onto the earth's parched surface each

The Maize god rises up from a split turtle shell, representing the barren earth, flanked by two manifestations of Chahk, the Storm god. The Lightning god K'awiil emerges from the right end of the carapace.

The Maize god sprouts from a skull-like, supernatural seed to emerge from a crack in a large turtle shell, accompanied by Juun Ajaw (left) and Yax Baluun (right).

season, to be revived by the rains. He steps lightly and sways like a supple, green maize plant to signal the start of a new generation. It is thanks to the Maize god's recurring sacrifice, death, rebirth, and resurgence that the Maya, who are both dependent upon and responsible for caring for him, can live.

CHAPTER 4

LIFE, DEATH, AND THE BEGINNINGS OF MAIZE AGRICULTURE

The Maize god's lifecycle mirrors that of not only the maize plant and milpa but also the cosmos itself. Born from a seed in the watery underworld, the Maize god grows into a robust adult before he is sacrificed and returns to the underworld. After death and burial, he is regenerated from a seed, sprouting up from the earth to begin the sequence anew. Renewal is always preceded by death and destruction. Without this end, as violent as it may be, rejuvenation is impossible. Thus, to plant, tend, and harvest maize is to escort the deity through another lifecycle, and to consume maize is to consume the body of the ancestors.

The Maize god's timeless lifecycle demonstrates that Classic Maya concepts of rebirth and renewal did not focus on the one-time transformation of a single individual or ancestor. The most salient value, which persists in many Maya communities today, is intergenerational renewal. One does not die and become an ancestor to achieve immortality; the goal is not to prolong one's individual experience, whether in this world or beyond. Instead, an ancestor's death necessarily paves the way for the life of a future generation by feeding back into the stuff—maize—from which the Maya themselves are made. For this reason, the word for "youth" or "young person" in the language of the Classic Maya hieroglyphs, as in many modern Mayan languages today, is the same as the word for "sprout." In other words, the Maize god represents not only the source of life for Maya peoples but also their individual and collective trajectories.

The Classic Maya myth of the Maize god's perpetual cycle of birth, sacrifice, and rejuvenation clearly attests that the plant was and remains

Detail of sarcophagus lid of K'inich Janaab Pakal II of Palenque, Chiapas, Mexico. The deceased king, in the guise of the youthful Maize god, reclines atop an underworld incense burner as the World Tree, with the Principal Bird Deity perched on top, rises above him.

a staple both agriculturally and culturally. As we have seen, maize frequently plays a minor role in other Maya myths, too. How, though, did the Maya acquire maize to begin with? How did the ancestors discover the crop and begin to cultivate and consume it? What does that origin account tell us about the social role that maize would continue to play among their descendants? One of the myriad Maya myths concerning the ancient ancestors' discovery of maize originates from the Mam town of Santiago Chimaltenango in the Department of Huehuetenango, Guatemala, during the first half of the twentieth century. In addition to illustrating how the ancestors obtained maize from a sacred mountain in the region, it explains humans' relationships with several animal companions that persist to this day.

The Ancestors Discover Maize

According to the Mam myth, there was no maize when humanity was first created. But Dios (God) wanted the people to have maize, a plant that seemed to be growing in a cleft in the mountain known as Paaxil, the abode of the Owner of Maize. Day in and day out, Dios observed a wildcat entering the opening, presumably to feast on maize, and leaving satisfied.

To obtain maize for the people, Dios called upon a louse, which he sent to fetch the plant to bring back from Paaxil. The next time the wildcat passed through on the way to the mountain, the louse

---

The Mountain of Maize

Local accounts vary in identifying the mountain homeland of maize. A roughly contemporaneous Mam tale from Colotenango, a town less than 8 km (5 miles) northeast of Santiago Chimaltenango, locates Paaxil in the municipality of La Libertad in the Department of Huehuetenango, some 20 km (12.5 miles) northwest of Colotenango. Another version of the myth from Todos Santos Cuchumatán, a Mam town 11 km (7 miles) northeast of Santiago Chimaltenango and 16 km (10 miles) northeast of Colotenango, describes the first people as receiving maize from a mountain named Xepaxá in San Pedro Necta, another Mam village about 17 km (10.5 miles) west of Todos Santos Cuchumatán and 7.5 km (4.5 miles) northwest of Colotenango. There is a long tradition of people journeying to Xepaxá to leave offerings as a petition for a good harvest, especially during an unfavorable agricultural season. Even now, when the Mam people run out of seed corn, they return to Xepaxá, where one can still find maize that grows wild on the mountain but also thrives when cultivated in the milpa.

A Classic Maya stucco model of a skeletal insect with a supernatural face from Tonina, Chiapas, Mexico.

clambered onto its back and held on tight to its fur. In this way, the little insect was able to enter the cleft in the mountain. But the louse fell asleep and did not wake up in time to see whether there was indeed any maize inside.

Since the louse did not fulfill its mission, Dios called upon another insect. But it did not bring back the maize that Dios wanted, either. So, Dios enlisted a flea, which successfully entered Paaxil and found the place where maize was stored. However, the flea was too small and weak to carry back any maize for Dios to give to the people. It could only report on the plant's location. To this day, fleas cling to the human torso, and especially to the area near the heart, because of the service that they performed for these early ancestors in locating maize.

"Mother Maize" in Colotenango

The Colotenango narrative provides more details about life before maize and an alternative account of who initiated the mission to the sacred mountain. In the primordial age before the milpa, it says, the people nourished themselves with the root of a plant with one stalk called *txetxina* or *txii'nan*, "mother maize." Txetxina root was their only sustenance until one day, they stumbled across a pile of dung from a mountain cat and noticed that it contained strange seeds. Unlike people today, the ancestors were able to talk directly with the animals with whom they shared the land. Thus, they sought out the feline and asked where it had obtained the food, and if it would be willing to show them the place. Instead, the mountain cat suggested that someone should join it on the next journey to the place where it went to eat. Thus, it was at the wildcat's suggestion that the people sent the louse to find the place of maize on the feline's back.

Finally, Dios called upon an army of ants, which went into Paaxil to fetch the maize. But the army failed to bring Dios an entire ear of corn, because it was too much for the slender insects to carry. Instead, each ant could transport only a single kernel of corn. This small amount was not enough for the people to plant. However, even today, the people pay their dues to the ants by allowing them to eat some maize in the milpa each season.

Dios shared the kernels that the ants had brought from Paaxil with the people, and taught them how to cultivate the plants and to cook and eat ripened corn. He taught them to gather seed corn from the feces of the wildcat that he had observed for so long eating maize in the cleft in the mountain. After the people's first crop of maize yielded only two ears of corn per stalk, Dios also instructed the people how to cultivate the milpa properly, so that they could increase their harvest.

A Late Classic ceramic sculpture of the Maya Maize god emerging from a husk or flower, perhaps from Jaina Island, Campeche, Mexico.

After the first ancestor cultivated his milpa under Dios's guidance, he harvested the inaugural ears to bring home to his family. He gave the corn to his wife and instructed her that she only needed to cook one kernel for the family. The wife did as she was told, and when she put the kernel in the pot, she saw how it expanded greatly in size, so that it was plenty for everyone. Thus, day after day, the wife only needed one kernel to prepare a single meal for the whole family. These first ancestors had an easy time of it because they needed so little maize to eat; as a result, the man did not have to grow many plants at all in his milpa.

Woodpeckers at Paaxil

The version of this story from Colotenango does not mention ants. Instead, the ancestors themselves went to Paaxil to find the maize. They peered into the cleft and saw that maize grew abundantly there, but the opening was too narrow for them to enter. They asked some red-headed woodpeckers if they would help them by using their beaks to widen the entrance. The woodpeckers went to work, and soon enough, the ancestors were able to enter Paaxil and bring maize back with them to plant in their fields.

The carefree time was not to last. When it came time for the first ancestor's son to find a wife, the woman whom he married proved to be difficult and opinionated, and she did not always listen to her husband or parents-in-law. One day, she cooked several kernels in the pot instead of just one, as her husband had instructed her to do. She wanted to cook more because, she said, there was no reason to be so miserly with their maize. Because of this first daughter-in-law's disobedience, however, the single kernels no longer expanded to fill up the pot as they had before. The people have a much more difficult life today because they need at least two pounds of maize to prepare each meal. The men must labor hard to cultivate large milpas, and the women must spend much of their time and energy cooking maize for their families each day.

Reciprocity in the Milpa

The Mam myth from Santiago Chimaltenango and related tales from neighboring towns about the origin of maize and the milpa emphasize ancient ties to specific locations that are still accessible to descendant communities today. It also illustrates the interdependence of human and other-than-human beings, especially animals, in the establishment of subsistence agriculture. The final myth in this chapter, a late twentieth-century K'iche' oral history from the region of Nahualá-Santa Catarina Ixtahuacán in Sololá, Guatemala, illustrates how the same reciprocal relations continue to define the milpa across the Maya region today. Over millennia, Maya farmers have been cosmologically obligated to engage with the gods responsible for sending the rains and sunshine needed for their crops to grow, and with the animals that venture into their fields. They have also learned to manage relationships with their crops, which require human respect and care to flourish. No matter how favorable the rains or how fertile the soil, Maya farmers always reap from the milpa what they sow.

A woman shucking and shelling maize in the municipality of Aguacatán, Huehuetenango, Guatemala.

From Foraging to Farming in Todos Santos Cuchumatán

Like the Colotenango version, the myth from Todos Santos Cuchumatán ascribes the adoption of maize to the ancestors themselves, with no divine guidance. However, it indicates that the people were slower to adopt agriculture than the other Mam narratives would suggest. Before the ancestors discovered corn, so the story goes, they subsisted on roots and fruits from the trees. One day, a man went to Xepaxá in pursuit of food. As he bent to the

Consagración del Maíz (Blessing of the Corn), 2005, by Pedro Rafael González Chavajay, a Tz'utujil painter from San Pedro La Laguna, Sololá, Guatemala.

Maize and Coffee's Flight

Some time ago, the residents of a small village found themselves facing food shortages after their maize and coffee crops did not produce the usual yields. In response to the impending famine, the government selected a cohort of local men to investigate the unproductive

ground to lay a trap to snare birds for meat, he noticed a young, green maize plant. He did not know what the strange stalk was, but he supposed that the kernels on the cob could be edible. He brought the maize down the mountain and back to his home, where the family members debated what to do with the curiosity. Should they eat it raw? Boil it? Roast it on hot coals? Finally, the man's wife decided to prepare it over the fire. The cooked kernels of the young ear of corn, still warm in their mouths, tasted delicious to them all.

Thus, the man returned the next day to Xepaxá to bring home more maize for his family to eat. He returned the day after that, too, and the day after that. After carrying the ripe cobs home, he shucked the corn and laid the kernels out to dry. But as he continued foraging at Xepaxá, the maize became sparser, and he had to venture farther and farther up the mountain to find it. He worried that he could be attacked, killed, and eaten by a wild animal, especially because mist often shrouded the mountain.

The man decided it was best to end his daily foraging trips. It would be better to search for a seed to plant on his own land, nearer to his house, so that they could raise the crop there. On his last ascent to Xepaxá, the man found a dried ear, which he planted near his home. There, the maize sprouted and grew taller and taller. He worked hard to cultivate the land so that the plant would thrive, and the new plant yielded many ears of fresh corn. Other people saw the crop and adopted it, and the custom of cultivating maize was passed down to their descendants. Thus, this ancestor established the practice of milpa that continues throughout the region today.

crops. Their mission required them to journey to a distant location. Unbeknownst to them, that place would turn out to be "the center of maize food" (K'iche' *ri uk'u'x ri wa*, literally "heart of maize food").

The community representatives traveled to Guatemala City and boarded a plane, carrying a letter from the government that explained

A dwarf kneels before a seated lord holding a cup in his palm in a Late Classic drawing from the Naj Tunich cave complex in Petén, Guatemala.

their mission to retrieve the maize and coffee plants. When they disembarked, they found themselves in an unfamiliar and rather desolate place, with just two houses, one woman, and no sign of anyone else. The party approached the lone woman and inquired about a man whom they had been told to meet. He was still out working in his fields, she said, so the visitors would have to wait.

Finally, the man returned home and asked the group awaiting him what had brought them there. "What is your errand? Tell me!" The visitors explained that they needed to speak with him, and presented the letter explaining their quest. After reviewing the paper, the man invited them into his home. He guided the strangers to a window and told them to look at the milpa outside. The fields were bursting with growing plants, but the visitors immediately noted that the crops seemed to be in bad shape and were crying out.

"What are they doing?" the host asked rhetorically. Without waiting for an answer, he revealed that they were the visitors' crops, in fact, which had suffered greatly because the farmers did not keep their fields clear of weeds to allow the crops to thrive. The abuse not only offended the crops, to which the host referred deferentially as "our mother" (K'iche' *qanaan*), but also caused them pain and had driven them to seek refuge in the center of maize food. There, far away from the negligent community, they knew that they would be treated with dignity.

Confronted with their shortcomings, the visitors realized that they were responsible for the poor harvest that was causing so much hardship. They were filled with regret for the distress that they had caused to their crops and, by extension, to their hungry community.

The host was not finished with his presentation, however. He proceeded to explain the specific complaints of the community's two most important crops, maize and coffee. The coffee beans ached from being roasted, ground, and mixed with hot water. They cried

A group harvesting coffee beans on the plantation Finca San Isidro in Mazatenango, Suchitepéquez, Guatemala, 1875.

out, he said, when they landed on the hot *comal* (griddle). They wailed as they were being reduced to powder, and again when they were spooned into the boiling water. The coffee beans felt as if they were being punished.

Maize had a different objection. It did not protest its means of preparation, which included being soaked in limewater, ground, and cooked over a fire. Instead, maize was offended that its tortillas were being consumed directly before hot coffee. The sequence not only burned the maize but "really blacken[ed] the bones of our mother" with the dark liquid.

Coffee and maize were both deeply unhappy with the community's practices, but they could not agree on a solution. Coffee claimed that it was not at fault for burning the maize; it was merely a victim of the community's wrongdoing. Coffee suggested that perhaps the people could consume the two foodstuffs separately, eating the maize first and following with the hot beverage. Maize countered that they should only eat its products. The coffee, maize said, should be sold at a profit instead of being drunk, and the farmers should use the income to buy other goods.

Maize had a third complaint to air. Traditionally, local farmers had planted a diverse range of maize varieties. Recently, however, some had developed a preference for cultivating and eating white maize, the most common variety on the global market. The rejection had wounded "the spirit of yellow maize ... the spirit of purple maize," causing much lamentation in the milpa. The colorful maize varieties had fled to their homeland to escape the humiliation of white maize's dominance.

Finally, the visitors fully understood the extent of the problems that they had caused by mistreating their crops, especially maize

A Late Classic ceramic figurine of a Maya woman rolling a grindstone (*mano*) atop a mealing stone (*metate*), perhaps processing corn.

and coffee. Their host and guide concluded his instructions by revealing that he was the spirit or lord of maize himself. His status had allowed him to mediate successfully between the crops and the community representatives, who could now return home from the center of maize food.

The Deal with the Weeds

A late twentieth-century Tsotsil tale from San Juan Chamula, Chiapas, Mexico, provides another perspective on the Maya's mutually sustaining relationship with maize and milpa agriculture. One day long ago, according to the Tsotsil storyteller, some ancestors were hoeing their milpa when they heard unfamiliar voices. They paused their work and walked toward the noise, searching for its source. They found no one, so they resumed their work among the rows of fledgling maize plants.

Later that afternoon, the ancestors passed an unknown man on the road. The stranger asked where they were coming from. The men responded that they had been working in the milpa and were now heading home. The stranger then asked if they had heard voices while working in the field. Surprised, they said yes, saying that it had seemed as if there were people talking, but no one was there.

The stranger commented that he, too, had once heard those voices. They belonged to the weeds, he said, who were complaining to Our Father Sun in Heaven about the abuse from the farmers' hoeing. The weeds had shed tears, afraid that they were being killed. It was unfair, they claimed, because they were being cut down to make room for the maize plants. Thus, they were trying to kill the maize by growing over the milpa.

As he told the ancestors, though, the stranger had made a deal with the weeds. He said that they must submit to being hoed and cut down in order to let the maize grow. However, he assured them, the weeds would not die but would instead be able to grow back each time. Since the agreement, the stranger said, the weeds had ceased protesting. He no longer heard their voices in the milpa.

Having wrapped up his own story, the stranger told the ancestors that the weeds in their milpa needed to be hoed because they had, in his words, "killed my body in the past, and might also kill me today." He admonished them that, although the weeds deserved to be cut down, the ancestors were ultimately responsible for carrying out that work and protecting the stranger from the weeds. Thus, they should continue to hoe the milpa, despite protest from the weeds. The men agreed and resumed their walk home.

The next day, and for every day after, the ancestors persisted in weeding their cornfields, ignoring the weeds' complaints. What the ancestors did not realize is that the stranger who had met them on the road that afternoon was actually Our Father Sun in Heaven himself—a divine being whose body is made of corn. So, when Tsotsil farmers hoe their milpas to clear weeds and to make room for their maize plants, they say, "We are defending the body of Our Father Sun."

PEOPLE OF MAIZE

Through centuries of religious and social transformation in the Maya region, maize remains the cultural heart of Indigenous subsistence. Even among families that no longer farm milpa, maize products remain the staple of meals. Traditional belief holds that the first ancestors were shaped from maize; thus, one must consume maize if one is to be Maya and to speak a Mayan language. As the K'iche' and Tsotsil myths about the milpa reveal, maize still represents a moral anchor for Maya communities, guiding interactions with other-than-human beings and among each other. Globalizing forces like the rise of cash cropping of coffee and other non-maize agricultural products, as well as an influx of cheap imported corn, continue to shape how Maya communities relate to the domesticate that their ancestors have been cultivating and consuming for millennia. Even these changes, however, are unlikely to displace

Abuelita Xmucane (Grandma Xmucane), 2008, by María Elena Curruchiche, a Kaqchikel painter from San Juan Comalapa, Chimaltenango, Guatemala.

maize's unique role as the agricultural cornerstone of Maya society anytime soon.

This is not to say that the Maya are rooted, immobile, to the fields whose fruits sustain them. The Maya have not always occupied the territories that they call home today. Archaeological, ethnohistorical, and historical linguistic evidence points to a long history of mobility and relocation across the region that stretches from pre-colonial into modern times. The intergenerational legacy of migration is reflected in the stories that different Maya groups tell about themselves as descendants of those whom ancestral leaders guided across strange, often challenging landscapes. These taxing journeys shaped the identity of each community as it searched for and eventually settled into its respective homeland. They also justified the authority of local nobility and rulers based on primordial precedent and literal and symbolic ties to a far-off center of power.

5

ORIGINS AND MIGRATION

Maya origin accounts consistently locate their primordial homeland somewhere far away, in many cases to the east, across a great sea. As among other Mesoamerican groups, Maya narratives of ancestral beginnings are defined by an epic migration out of that homeland. After much suffering and wandering through a difficult landscape, the mass of undifferentiated ancestors that had departed the homeland together gradually fissioned into distinct ethnolinguistic groups. Their leaders distinguished themselves during the migration and bore with them the seminal emblems of rulership whose inheritance defined patterns of succession among their descendants.

Archaeological, genetic, and textual information attest to a core truth underlying these myths of primordial migration, namely that the ancient Maya were highly mobile, as were other Mesoamerican peoples. Travelers and traders constantly traversed the region, crossing even the most challenging landscapes on foot without beasts of burden to lighten their load. Populations also relocated in response to many of the same factors that still drive migration today, including changing weather patterns, natural disaster, violent conflict, or the promise of a better life just beyond the horizon. Despite scholars' attempts to identify a primordial Maya homeland, many locations described in the myths probably do not correspond to physical places on the Mesoamerican landscape. The chronology and trajectory of Maya migration is also unlikely to have been as straightforward as the origin stories suggest.

K'ICHE'AN MIGRATION FROM ACROSS THE SEA

Based on hieroglyphic (pre-colonial) and alphabetic sources, it is clear that the basic contours of the Maya origin narrative—distant homeland, migration after accepting symbols of rulership, crossing a great sea—originated at least a millennium before European contact. From the many dozens of Maya origin myths that have been recorded, two versions are especially rich in detail. Both originate from highland Guatemala and were probably first written down in the sixteenth century, yet they represent distinct points of view. Together, they illustrate a tension between regional similarities and local differences that characterizes narratives of Maya origins more generally, including those still being told today.

Xajil Chronicle

According to a Kaqchikel source known today as the *Memorial of Sololá* or the *Xajil Chronicle*, the first people originated in a primordial homeland, Pa Tulan, far away from their current territory in the Guatemalan highlands. In this early world, there were four Pa Tulans: one in the east, one in the west, one in the zenith (the highest point of the sun's daily journey), and one in the nadir (underworld). The Kaqchikel and other highland Maya peoples were created in the western Pa Tulan. It was there that they gave birth to the first ancestors.

The first people lived a difficult life. They had no maize or agriculture. They ate only dirt, wood, and leaves. They could not walk or talk. They did not even have flesh or blood. It was not until the coyote and the crow brought the first kernels that they had maize. A sparrowhawk brought blood from the *tixlikumätz*, an ocean serpent.

Tulan as the Maya Homeland

Many Maya peoples ascribe their origins to a distant place, often said to be in the east across a large sea, and this trope is probably original to the Maya. The specific identification of this far-off homeland as Tulan, however, was probably adopted from central Mexico. The toponym is itself a Maya rendering of Nahuatl *Tōllān*, which means "Place of Cattail Reeds" and denoted any of a number of places believed to have been sites of creation, including Teotihuacan, Tenochtitlan, Tula, and Chichen Itza. In central Mexican cosmology, Tōllāns were not only places where ancestors emerged; they were also pilgrimage destinations where those ancestors' descendants journeyed to be invested with emblems of rulership.

The Postclassic Maya probably equated their primordial homeland with Tōllān in response to the political and cultural prestige of Postclassic central Mexican civilization. By locating their ancestors' origins in a homeland that was not only far away and foreign but also shared with the mighty Toltecs, Aztecs, and other powers in central Mexico, they legitimized their own authority at home. Thus, references to Tulan as the place of Maya origin are best interpreted as metaphors, rather than as indicating a specific locale on the Mesoamerican landscape.

Mixing the maize with the liquid blood, the creators—a pair of complementary gods known as Tz'aqol B'itol and Alom K'ajolom—kneaded a dough from which they shaped the true ancestors, thirteen men and fourteen women.

Unlike the first people, these ancestors could walk and talk. They were farmers and were made of blood and flesh, just like we are today. The first ancestors joined with each other to create new ancestors. The entrance to Tulan was covered by a bat, however, so that the ancestors could not pass through.

On a dark night after they had begun to multiply, the ancestors received their burdens. The patron gods bestowed upon them sacred bundles, which were both a physical weight and a moral responsibility for the bearers. By then, the ancestors had divided into seven *amaq's* and thirteen divisions of warriors. The seven amaq's lined up in the left side of Tulan, while the warriors stood ready in the right side. That is how they received their burdens from the first fathers and mothers.

The burdens of the seven amaq's were green-blue jade; brilliant feathers from quetzals, trogons, and scarlet macaws; precious metals; flutes; white clay; upright stone stelae; and cacao pods and beans. The seven amaq's also received the first writing, carving, weaving, music, and the 260-day and solar calendars. The ancestors accepted all these material and cultural riches to carry with them from Tulan.

An altar from Caracol, Cayo District, Belize, records a meeting at Ucanal, Petén, Guatemala, in 817 between K'inich Toobil Yopaat (right), king of Caracol, and Papmalil (left), a foreigner ruling at Ucanal.

Highland Maya Social Organization

Scholars have yet to fully disentangle the complex structure of Postclassic highland Maya society, but the general contours are reasonably clear. The second most basic component of society, just above the level of the family, was the clan, called the *chinamit* or *calpul*, the latter term borrowed from Nahuatl *calpulli*. Rather than a kinship-based lineage, the chinamit appears to have been a unit of territorial organization governed by a leading noble family that the commoner chinamit members supported with tribute and labor. An *amaq'* was a confederation of multiple chinamits that probably lived on neighboring lands and may have intermarried, at least in the case of noble families. Amaq's allied or confederated as a single *winäq* or *winaq* ("nation, people") or polity, the largest unit of highland Maya sociopolitical organization. The Postclassic polity based at Chi Iximche', for instance, was governed by the Kaqchikel winäq, which by the end of the fifteenth century consisted of two amaq's of four chinamits each. The polity centered at Q'umarkaaj, in turn, was ruled by the K'iche' winaq, which had three component amaq's, each with its own subsidiary chinamits.

The warriors, for their part, received bows and arrows and rounded shields to carry on their migration.

The first fathers and mothers told the ancestors to take up their burdens and leave Tulan, and that they would cross a great sea to find their homelands amid the mountains and valleys on the other side of the water. The first fathers and mothers instructed that the ancestors should bring their burdens and display them as signs of their power. With the emblems, each amaq' could come into its lordship and occupy its canopied throne. Only after the ancestors had received their burdens was the entrance to Tulan unsealed to allow them to pass through.

Courtiers at Late Classic Bonampak, Chiapas, Mexico, proffer to their seated ruler a headband, known as *sak hu'n* ("white paper"), symbolizing divine kingship. The act of "holding up" or "raising" the *sak hu'n* was a common component of Classic Maya accession ceremonies.

The seven amaq's were the first to leave Tulan, led by the Tz'utujil, with the Kaqchikel bringing up the rear. Then came the thirteen divisions of warriors. They were led by the K'iche', who carried with them the Aztec ceremony of Xipe Toltec, in which fighters donned the flayed skins of sacrificial victims in ritual battle. After the K'iche' came the Rab'inal, the Sotz'il, and the Tuquche'. Marching behind them were the Tujalajay, the Uchab'ajay, and the Ch'umilajay; they were followed by the Lamaq', the Kumätz, the Aqajal, and the Tukur. The B'akaj was the last division of ancestors to leave Pa Tulan.

Thus, the seven amaq's set off on the great migration with the counsel of their elders ringing in their ears: Go forth, bringing your glittering burdens to your homelands. Carry them with dignity, show them with pride, and you will receive the canopy and throne

Kaqchikel warriors fight with bows, arrows and round shields against Spanish and Tlaxcalan invaders at Chi Iximche' in 1524. Scene 79 of the *Lienzo de Tlaxcala*, *c.* 1552.

of lordship. "May you never be disrespected; but rather may you become great!" the first fathers and mothers called after them. They implored the thirteen warrior divisions to use their bows and arrows and shields to take control of their territories.

From the very beginning, the ancestors suffered on their migration. They were stung by bees and wasps. The sun hid behind clouds as the travelers waded through mud, fog, and rain after leaving Pa Tulan. Ominous signs appeared along their path. A roadrunner predicted that they would be lost and die; an owl and a hawk prophesied the same fate. But the ancestors steeled themselves against the bad omens. Your words are not prophecies, the ancestors responded to the avian observers; they are merely your bird calls. That is why these winged creatures send the same message to us today from their perch up in the trees.

The ancestors soon arrived at the shore of a great sea. Six of the seven amaq's and all thirteen warrior divisions stopped at the edge of the water, wringing their hands as they realized that there was no way to cross the vast expanse before them. If they were unable to cross the sea, they could not realize the destinies that they had been given upon leaving Pa Tulan, the destinies symbolized by the burdens that they carried on their backs. What should we do, they wondered? The ancestors were overwhelmed by the challenge before them. Engulfed by despair, they lay down on the sandy shore.

As the final amaq' to leave Pa Tulan and the last to arrive at the great waters, the Kaqchikels found a scene of dismay when they caught up to the other peoples. Two Kaqchikel ancestors, Q'aq'awitz and Saktekaw, rallied all the people to take heart. It was not their fate to give up here, they said, for beyond the waters lay the homelands where they were meant to arrive. Q'aq'awitz and Saktekaw seized the staff of the red tree, the *kaqache'*, that they had brought with them from Pa Tulan as the Kaqchikel people's emblem. They stabbed its wooden base into the waves, and to the others' amazement, the waters immediately parted. A sandy path opened where they had previously seen only the sea's undulating surface.

Overcome with joy and relief, the amaq's and warriors followed the seabed road until they reached the opposite shore. The Kaqchikels were the last amaq' to emerge from the sea, and they joined the other peoples who had gathered on a nearby hill. It was on that hilltop that the first major division of the ancestors took place, as the seven amaq's decided to part ways with the warriors. Instead of joining the warriors on their march to the east, the seven amaq's said, they would strike out on their own to find the homelands about which they had been told in Pa Tulan. Having successfully crossed the great sea together, the ancestors continued along their own paths. Thus began the differentiation that would, over the course of many generations, produce the diverse political confederations and sociolinguistic groups inhabiting the sixteenth-century Guatemalan highlands.

Title of Totonicapán

Another source, known today as the *Title of Totonicapán*, was penned in the colonial town after which it is named in 1554, around the same time as the *Xajil Chronicle*. Similar to their Kaqchikel counterparts, the K'iche' authors of the *Title of Totonicapán* identified the first people's primordial homeland as a faraway location known as Pa Sewan and Pa Tulan. It was there, they wrote, that the people had their origins and from there that they derived their power and might.

Still, Pa Sewan and Pa Tulan was no idyllic paradise. Some of the ancestors' traditions were misguided. In particular, they venerated the sun and the moon. To them, the planetary bodies represented male and female beings, respectively (see Chapter 2). They also believed that the sun and moon embodied the precocious Hero Twins from the *Popol Vuh*, Junajpu' and Xb'alanke' (see Chapter 3). In the stars, in turn, they saw the lit cigars of the gods smoking in the heavens above. The ancestors were, in fact, the sons and daughters of Moses, Israelites who had already departed Babylonia in the east. They traced their origins to the great Nakxit, the primordial lord from whom they were descended. The early people were wise and all-knowing, aware of all that happened across the face of the earth.

It came time for the ancestors, the seven amaq's and the ancestral clans, to depart Pa Sewan and Pa Tulan, the place where the sun ascended into the sky. The first amaq', the K'iche', were guided by

Tz'utujil women from Santiago Atitlán, Sololá, Guatemala, fill their ceramic jars with water from Lake Atitlán, 1930s.

four principal ancestors. The first lord, B'alam K'itze', and his wife, Kaqapaluma, founded the Kaweq chinamit. The Nija'ib' chinamit was descended from the second lord, B'alam Aq'ab', and his wife, Sunija. Majukotaj was third in line and originator of the Ajaw K'iche' chinamit, together with Kaqixaja, his wife. The fourth, Ik'i B'alam,

On a Late Preclassic monument from Kaminaljuyu', an archaeological site now under Guatemala City, half-naked captives kneel before enthroned persons whose unique headdresses may denote the wearers' names.

A "Theology for/of the Indians"

When the first Catholic missionaries arrived in the Maya region in the early sixteenth century, they faced the imposing task of converting thousands of people, speaking dozens of languages, to a completely foreign religion. A key strategy for confronting this challenge was translating Catholic myths and tenets into Mayan languages. An early pioneer in these efforts was Domingo de Vico, a Dominican friar from Spain who completed the two-volume *Theologia Indorum* by 1554. Vico most likely wrote his "Theology for/of the Indians" in K'iche', with support from Indigenous consultants and co-authors, and the text was later translated into other highland Mayan languages. Its contents were never published, but nevertheless circulated widely in the region and informed religious thought among generations of missionary and Maya audiences alike. Those audiences included the authors of both the *Popol Vuh*, who responded by composing their own treatise on Maya cosmology, and the *Title of Totonicapán*, who integrated excerpts from Vico's *Theologia Indorum* into their own text to demonstrate the compatibility of Judeo-Christian and Maya thought.

was too young to marry when they departed Pa Tulan and left no descendant lineage.

When they departed Pa Sewan and Pa Tulan, the four founders and their partners were followed by the Tamub', another amaq' of the K'iche' nation. They were led by four progenitors to whom later Tamub' leaders traced their origins: K'opichoch, K'ochojlan, Majk'inalom, and K'oq'anawil. It is from them that the two major Tamub' chinamits, K'aqoj and Eq'omaq', are descended. With the Tamub' came another K'iche' amaq', the Ilokab', headed by six leaders of their own. Chiya' Toj, Chiya' Tz'ikin, Yol Chitum, Yol Chiramaq', Ch'ipel Kan, and Muq'el Kan led the Ilokab' out from Pa Sewan and

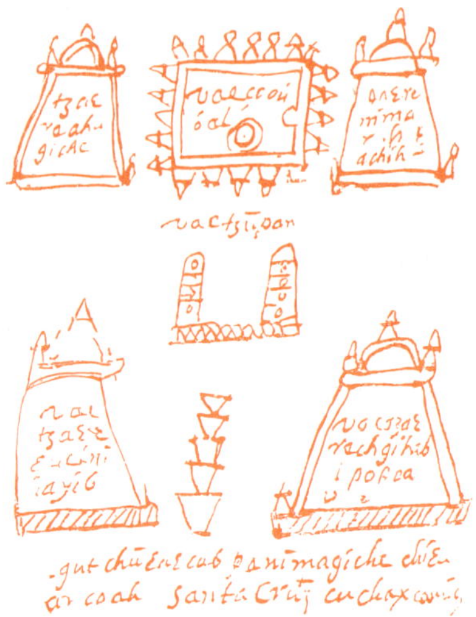

Sketch of the ceremonial center of Q'umarkaaj from the *Title of Totonicapán* (fol. i), showing the four temples at the corners and a sacrificial space (top center) around a skull rack in the middle of the plaza.

Pa Tulan. They were the originators of the three primary chinamits of the Ilokab': Q'ale, Sik'a, and Juwanija.

All three amaq's—the Tamub', the Ilokab', and the K'iche'—were united in the K'iche' nation by a shared language and identity. They were the children of Israel who had come to Pa Sewan and Pa Tulan from Babylonia in the east. When leaving Pa Sewan and Pa Tulan, the ancestors bore a sacred burden that lord Nakxit had bestowed upon them. They were dressed only in leaves and, other than the divine bundle, carried with them only spears.

The amaq's arrived at the edge of a great sea. There, the first K'iche' lord, B'alam K'itze', grasped his wooden staff and thrust it into the water's surface. Suddenly, the contents of the great sea vanished, leaving behind only a bed of sand. Thus, the three K'iche' amaq's were able to cross to the opposite shore. The thirteen clans and seven amaq's traversed the dry sea floor. Once they had all reached the other side, the waters flowed back into place behind them, and the sandy path that they had taken disappeared. Their safe passage had been a gift from Tz'aqol B'itol, their one god at the heart of the sky and the earth. Tz'aqol B'itol loved the ancestors, who were the children of Abraham.

Having reached the other side of the ocean, the ancestors continued the migration together. They suffered hunger and deprivation. Although they briefly rested at landmarks along the way, their journey continued across many mountains. At one station, the four K'iche' progenitors—B'alam K'itze', B'alam Aq'ab', Majukotaj, and Ik'i B'alam—lit the first fire. The seven amaq's and thirteen clans, however, were unable to create fire. They begged the K'iche' lords to share their fire with them. In return, they agreed to sacrifice their hearts to the lords. Their submission represented the first sacrifice of the ancestors.

After the first sacrifice, the ancestors parted ways. Atop the mountain that they had named Jaqawitz Ch'ipaq, the leaders of the various groups held counsel and agreed to continue their journeys separately. From there, the Tamub', Ilokab', other amaq's and thirteen clans set out toward different mountains. They left behind B'alam K'itze', B'alam Aq'ab', Majukotaj, and Ik'i B'alam, who established the ruling lineage of the K'iche' amaq' there atop Jaqawitz Ch'ipaq.

Complementary Perspectives

Despite its rich detail, the *Xajil Chronicle* does not present a comprehensive account of the highland Maya ancestors' primordial migration. Like any history, the text was shaped by the interests of its Kaqchikel authors, who were members of the Xajil chinamit that

The main plaza of San Cristóbal Totonicapán, Totonicapán, Guatemala, *c.* 1875.

traced its lineage back to Q'aq'awitz and Saktekaw themselves. It is no wonder that the narrative of the journey from Pa Tulan through the great sea prioritizes the Kaqchikel perspective and presents the Xajil ancestors in an especially favorable light.

The *Title of Totonicapán*'s account of the primordial migration is briefer, and contains many of the same tropes and basic ideas found in the *Xajil Chronicle*. However, it represents a K'iche' take on the shared primordial past, specifically the perspective of the Ajaw K'iche', Kaweq, and Nija'ib' chinamits whose leaders signed the colonial document. Unsurprisingly, the authors of the *Title of Totonicapán* emphasize their ancestors' roles in leading all the peoples out of Pa Tulan. The K'iche', rather than the Tz'utujil, are said to be the first to leave the primordial homeland. Instead of Q'aq'awitz and Saktekaw, it is B'alam K'itze', the first of the K'iche' progenitors, who parts the water of the great sea and leads the ancestors across the dry floor.

The texts do not contradict each other as much as they depict divergent perspectives on a shared history. Those who committed the *Xajil Chronicle* and the *Title of Totonicapán* to paper in the sixteenth century were writing within decades of the first encounter between biblical and Indigenous mythologies. Yet only the latter text directly engages with the new Catholic religion. Scattered biblical references reflect the *Title of Totonicapán* authors' very intentional effort to reconcile a K'iche' understanding of the ancestral past with the Judeo-Christian origin stories that Catholic missionaries introduced into highland Guatemala in the sixteenth century. Perhaps as part of this strategy, the *Title of Totonicapán* narrative contextualizes the first heart sacrifice—a practice that the Spaniards had banned as pagan barbarism—within the division of the first peoples after they had crossed the sea.

THE "TRUE PEOPLE": ONE MAYA COMMUNITY'S UNIQUE BEGINNINGS

The K'iche' and Kaqchikel narratives locate their peoples' origins in collective migration from a homeland far away from their territories in the highlands. A late twentieth-century Lacandón story, in contrast, illustrates the Lacandón's inception in a primordial union between human and avian ancestors. This feature may reflect the Lacandón's exceptional experience in the five hundred years that have passed since the advent of Spanish colonialism. They represent an ethnolinguistic group that took shape during the colonial period as members of different Maya groups fled from conquistadors, missionaries, and settlers deep into the subtropical forests

A Lacandón group at Lake Petha' (Laguna Guinea), Chiapas, Mexico, 1898.

of what are now the western Petén, Guatemala, and southeastern Chiapas, Mexico. By establishing dispersed, mobile communities in a forest into which most outsiders were loath to venture, the Lacandón maintained their culture, religion, and language—a close linguistic relative of Yucatec Maya—for generations with little outside interference.

As a result of this history, the Lacandón are the only Maya people to have escaped forced resettlement and religious conversion into the nineteenth century, having successfully limited outside contact primarily to trade. This equilibrium began to unbalance in the late nineteenth century, however, when non-Indigenous

Mexicans and, later, other Indigenous groups began migrating in large numbers to the lowlands of Chiapas. As loggers, ranchers, and other industrially minded settlers were lured to the largely untouched forests in the Lacandón's home region, the Lacandón—already a relatively small population due to their semi-nomadic lifestyle and kinship structure—were forced to retreat deeper and deeper into the jungle, and as the surrounding population grew and deforestation accelerated, they became less and less able to regulate outside influence, whether religious, economic, or epidemic, on their own terms.

Since at least the mid-twentieth century, the Lacandón have referred to themselves as *hach winik*, literally "true people." In the late twentieth century, the designation was reserved for those who still practiced traditional Lacandón religion, as opposed to Christianity. By the early twenty-first century, however, *hach winik* has become a straightforward ethnonym without religious connotations. Today, the Lacandón are among the culturally and linguistically most threatened Maya peoples, with an estimated population of fewer than 600.

What follows is a rendering of the Northern Lacandón myth about the origin of their people, with intermittent references to a cognate Southern Lacandón tale. Despite a common history and many cultural and linguistic similarities, the Northern and Southern Lacandón consider themselves fundamentally different communities. From the nineteenth through mid-twentieth centuries, they lived largely in isolation from each other in different areas of western Chiapas. Their distinct identities are mirrored in some narrative discrepancies in Northern and Southern Lacandón origin narratives. At the same time, the myth's basic contours reflect experiences and concerns shared by both groups. Perhaps most notable among them is that despite distinct kinship and marriage traditions, they have struggled for generations to find enough young, marriage-eligible women to maintain their communities.

The Origin of the *Hach Winik*, According to the Northern Lacandón

A long time ago, there were very few women among the people, so that men had to prepare their own food. Many men who desperately wanted to marry had to cast a wide net and search for eligible brides outside of the people.

One day, an ancestor was walking through the forest to gather copal when he stumbled across two female king vultures bathing in a stream. He observed in amazement as they removed their feather tunics to bathe, grasping limes in their hands. They looked very much like women as they stood there washing themselves, squeezing the

---

Copal

Mesoamericans have long used the dried resin of the copal tree, which is native to the region, and related species in the family *Burseraceae* as an incense. Burning the hardened sap emits a fragrant smoke and has been an integral component of Maya ritual practice for over two millennia. In Maya cosmology, copal is considered a basic food of the gods and ancestors, just as human blood was in ancient times. The *Popol Vuh*'s account in Chapter 3 of Ixkik', the Hero Twins' underworld mother who evaded sacrifice by substituting copal for her heart, offers a mythohistorical basis for this equivalence.

---

limes on their heads so that the juice ran down their bodies into the water swirling around them. As the ancestor watched from his hiding place, the women finished bathing, donned their feathers, and flew off into the sky.

The next day, the man returned to wait for the female vultures instead of going to work in the milpa. He had been wanting to find a wife and did not want to miss this opportunity. Moving quietly to the riverbank, he slipped into the water and swam toward the bathers undetected. Catching them by surprise, he succeeded in grabbing one of the vultures as her companion fled.

The vulture struggled against his grip and yelled at the stranger to let her go. "I don't have a wife," the ancestor told her. "Do you think that you'll be a good husband?" she countered. "You've seized me while I'm naked. What am I to wear? Will you give me clothing?" He assured her that he would. "Leave my feathers here," she instructed him. "My sister will come to fetch them later." So, the man brought the vulture home with him, where he gave her clothes that had belonged to his mother before she passed. Dressed in this manner, the vulture looked entirely like a human woman. The man married her, and they began a happy life together.

One day, about a year after their marriage, his wife invited the ancestor to visit the home of her parents and many other family members up in the sky. There, above the earth's surface, the vultures lived on a level of the heavens just below that of the creator. Her father, she told her husband, was the lord of the vultures, and was glad to know that his daughter had married. Back in those days, there was a path connecting the place of the vultures in the sky with the forest where the people lived. The couple was able to walk directly to visit her people, for the way was not very far at all.

Trophy Wife

According to the Southern Lacandón myth, the ancestor received a tunic from his mother, who was still alive and overjoyed that her son had finally found a wife. His parents were fascinated by the beautiful woman and did not leave her side when she first came to live with them. The neighbors also came to see the new bride and to admire her handsomeness. When his relatives asked where he had found her, he retorted, "I asked you to find me one, and none of you did so! You did not help me back then."

In the realm of the vultures, the ancestor observed many milpas full of waving, green maize plants. There were many people, too, and they looked very familiar to him. Indeed, they all seemed in his eyes to be more human than vulture. Instead of feathers, they were wearing tunics, just like the people below.

The ancestor met with his father-in-law, the lord of the vultures, whose mouth was filled with yellow teeth that stood out in stark contrast to his bald head. The vulture lord told the ancestor that because his wife was a vulture, his soul would not be taken by Kisin, the god of death who incinerated the people's souls in hell to absolve their sins. Instead, when the ancestor died, his soul would come to rest in the sky with the other vultures. No one knows whether the ancestor's soul really did escape Kisin's punishment after he died, however, because of how badly he behaved after returning home from the realm of the vultures.

Back among the people, the ancestor began mistreating his vulture-wife. He mocked her for eating rotten meat. His wife told him that the larvae wriggling in carrion were chilis on her tongue and tasted delicious. The description only disgusted her husband further. He hunted meat and brought it home for his wife to prepare. She always allowed the meat to decompose for a while before cooking it, so it tasted putrid to him and was filled with worms. Finally, the ancestor decided that he had had enough, and he abandoned his wife to live by herself in the house. "From now on," he told her, "you will eat alone." Instead of coming home to her, he began living in his milpa.

Some time after her husband had left her, the vulture-wife was visited by a *xok*, an aquatic being that is known for catching fish. They slept together, and the vulture became pregnant. The pregnancy made her ill, such that one day, when the ancestor finally decided to return home, he found his wife on the brink of death. After she

Cruzando Fronteras (Crossing Borders), 2007, by Paula Nicho Cúmez, a Kaqchikel painter from San Juan Comalapa, Chimaltenango, Guatemala.

confessed to him what had happened after he had abandoned her, she implored her husband to open her womb and get rid of the xok's unborn children. The ancestor found ten little crocodiles inside his wife, which he killed, as she had requested.

Yet the vulture-wife did not recover. As she lay dying, she instructed her husband to cut open her pinky finger. "There you will find little squash seeds," she told him. "Plant them in your milpa, for they are our daughters." She explained to her husband how to tend to the plants so that they would bear fruit. Just before passing away, she also told him to use his machete to clear the weeds around the fruit as it ripened, being careful to not slash the stems, and to cover the maturing fruit with leaves to protect them from dehydrating under the sun's strong rays. When they ripened, she continued, he should harvest the squashes and bring them home to put under the bench in the kitchen on which she usually ground maize.

The Vulture Learns to Eat Maize

The Southern Lacandón myth presents a different sequence of events. Soon after their marriage, the ancestor became frustrated with his new wife's preference for rotten meat, and despite his scolding, he could not convince her to eat corn instead. Desperate, he turned to the gods, lighting incense for them in the burners and begging them to make her eat like him and the rest of the people. The gods listened to his petition, and gradually, the woman began to eat tortillas. She started drinking atole and, eventually, became accustomed to eating all kinds of human food. It was only after that conflict was resolved that the couple went to visit the realm of the vultures.

A Lacandón woman weaves on a backstrap loom as four children look on, probably in Chiapas, Mexico, *c.* 1902–3.

The ancestor, who was not particularly sad after his wife's death, did exactly as she had instructed. He planted the seeds and tended them with care, watching as they sprouted, grew tendrils, and blossomed. In the meantime, he continued eating and living alone. By the end of the season, the healthy plants had yielded three plump fruits. The widower accidentally broke one as he harvested them, but managed to salvage the other two. He brought them home and placed them under the bench in the kitchen, exactly as his deceased wife had indicated.

The next day, when the ancestor came back to the house after gathering copal in the forest, he was astonished to find warm tortillas and atole awaiting him in the kitchen. The same mysterious presentation greeted him when he returned home the next day, and the next, after long hours working in the milpa. Each morning, he would leave his empty home and come back in the afternoon to food that had been prepared for him in his absence.

One day, the widower returned home a little earlier than usual from the milpa. When he entered the house, he was shocked to see two nude women in the kitchen, where they were grinding corn. They told him that they were his daughters who had grown inside the squashes. Every day, after their father left for the fields, each emerged from her gourd to prepare his food. They retreated to their hiding places just before he arrived back at the house. Surprised by the encounter with their father, they tried to cover their bare bodies

An Unsavory Homecoming

The Southern Lacandón account concludes with the return of the ancestor and his wife to earth from the realm of the vultures. There is no indication of how their family's story continues, but the very different experience of their visit to the heavens suggests a more harmonious conclusion than the Northern Lacandón tale.

The Southern Lacandón narrative claims that one day, after she had grown accustomed to eating maize like the people, the vulture-wife asked her mother-in-law to give her some cotton from which to weave a tunic for her husband to wear so that they could visit her father and mother. In fact, what the wife wove for her husband was a feathered vulture tunic that would allow him to fly. When she showed her husband the new tunic, he was initially reluctant to try out the wings. But she insisted that he put it on, and once she taught him how to take flight, the ancestor found that he truly enjoyed flying. Wearing the tunic, he looked very much like a king vulture himself.

Now that her husband could fly with his new outfit, the vulture-wife invited him to accompany her to the celestial realm of the vultures, where he could finally meet her father and mother. She

with their arms as they spoke to him. They ordered him to not come any closer until they could put on some clothing, asking if he still had the old garments that their mother had worn.

The ancestor brought his daughters the same clothes that he had once given his wife. Once they had dressed themselves, the women scolded their father for having mistreated their mother, the vulture. The ancestor cried as he remembered his misdeeds. After that day, the women did not return to their gourds. They stayed with their father and continued to cook for him, taking care of the house while he was out in the fields every day.

---

offered to put her mother-in-law on her back so that she could accompany them, too, but she refused because she was too afraid that she would fall off. Thus, the couple took off into the sky, leaving the ancestor's mother behind. On the way, the vulture-wife warned her husband that if any of her family members asked him if he had a thorn in his foot, he should not say anything. Above all, he should not show his foot, even if they offered to remove the thorn, because what they really wanted was to bite off his foot.

When the ancestor and his wife arrived at the home of his vulture in-laws, they were confronted by a foul odor emanating from the house because of all the rotting meat stored inside, which was scattered across the floor. The vulture-wife told her mother that her home smelled rancid. She refused to eat any carrion that her mother offered her, saying that the larvae disgusted her. Just as the vulture-wife had expected, her mother asked the ancestor if he had a thorn in his foot, but because he said no and refused her offer to look at it, no harm came to him. After the visit to the ancestor's mother-in-law in the realm of the vultures, husband and wife returned home to continue living among the people below on earth.

Eventually, a neighbor came by and asked the ancestor for his daughters' hands in marriage. The widower told him that he could not give away his daughters because without them, there would be no one to feed him, as his wife had died. The neighbor initially offered to allow the widower to marry one of his younger sisters, but hesitated as he remembered that the ancestor had not been a good husband to his daughters' mother. "Yes, it's true," the widower admitted, "but she was a vulture who ate carrion!" "And your daughters?" the neighbor asked with some concern. "They came from squashes," the ancestor assured him, explaining the story of their conception.

Finally, the two men reached an agreement, and the vulture's daughters left to marry the neighbor, while the ancestor welcomed another wife into his house. Although he died only a year later from a snakebite, his daughters had many children, grandchildren, even

A Lacandón woman prepares tortillas in Chiapas, *c.* 1946–47.

Luck or Divine Intervention?

Whereas the Northern Lacandón version of this story implies that the ancestor's encounter with the vulture women was a lucky break, the Southern Lacandón account credits the gods for the meeting. In that version, the ancestor initially asked his relatives to find him a wife, but they could not find a suitable woman. Growing hopeless, the ancestor turned to his incense burners with a petition to the gods. In response, the gods arranged for the man to encounter the female vultures as they bathed at the river, perched on a tree trunk as they washed themselves with clay.

great-grandchildren. That is why one should not kill vultures, because long ago, when there were not enough women, the gods allowed a vulture to transform into a human and to marry a man. She bore children who cared for their father and who later married and gave birth to children of their own, allowing the community to grow and prosper. But because the ancestor treated his vulture-wife so poorly before her death, the gods never again allowed a man to marry a vulture.

Kinship and the Ancestors

This Lacandón origin myth is not unique in portraying primordial unions between human and non-human ancestors. Other Lacandón tales describe ancestral men who, back in those early days when there were too few women to go around, married a monkey or peccary, among other animals. Collectively, these narratives account for a traditional Lacandón preference to marry among themselves, rather than with strangers. In particular, the Northern tale offers an ancestral justification for polygamy, including the relatively common practice of men in that group taking biological siblings as wives. As both versions of the Lacandón origin myth articulate, these marriage choices had very material consequences. The gendered cooperation described in the tales formed the foundation of traditional Maya subsistence for generation upon generation: men cultivate the milpa and hunt, women tend the garden and cook.

The Lacandón story of the ancestor and his vulture-wife also roots ancestral identity in maize, the foodstuff that was and remains the essence of Maya being (see Chapter 4). In both versions, maize is juxtaposed to other foodstuffs like meat and, in the Northern version, squash. Although humans and vultures alike eat meat, that food does not define the people in the same way that maize does, a fact that is illustrated most explicitly in the Southern version. Instead, the basic food and drink of Lacandón daily life are tortillas and atole. By sharing these maize dishes at meals together, day after day, Lacandón people affirmed their identity as a family unit and as *hach winik* of the forest.

The K'iche', Kaqchikel, and Lacandón origin myths account for the beginnings of ethnolinguistic communities, including principles of intermarriage and descent. They do not, however, explain more recent transformations in their respective sociopolitical or cultural identities. Maya mythohistory typically contextualizes such foundational events within the biographies of one or a handful of apical ancestors. Like the K'iche' and Kaqchikel progenitors, these persons tended to derive their power and strength from a distant land and were often foreigners themselves. Unlike the migrants leaving Tulan, however, the strangers' individual actions and the consequences thereof profoundly transformed the descendant community's identity. Their legacies were defined by a combination of mythohistorical narration and historiographical reinterpretation, as we will see in the next chapter.

6

FOUNDINGS

Collective origin stories like the ones presented in Chapter 5 root the narrating community's identity in a deep past shared with other Maya peoples. At the same time, they offer historical justification for the social, cultural, and political diversity that characterizes the Maya region into the present. They attribute existing power relations and their material symbolism to primordial events that the ancestors experienced in a faraway place and time. Ultimately, Maya myths about the origins of ancestral authority served an ideological purpose by legitimizing social structures that persisted among their descendants.

For the same reasons, however, the origin stories can be misinterpreted as implying a degree of historical isolation that likely never existed. With their emphasis on a primordial link between place and identity, the Lacandón, Kaqchikel, K'iche', and other ethnolinguistic origin myths could give the erroneous impression that Maya peoples, although diverse among themselves, developed independently from neighboring civilizations or regional sociopolitical events. Even with its title, this book seems to assume a hermetic "Maya" mythological tradition, perhaps related to but clearly divisible from other Mesoamerican traditions.

This assumption falls apart as one dives into the myths themselves, as we will see in this final chapter. It presents two tales about foreigners whose arrival to the region forever altered the arc of Maya mythohistory.

Both myths attest that phenomena such as dynastic founding, conquest, and sociopolitical transformation were not unique to the primordial past. They also underscore the extent to which Maya peoples, for all their distinctive commonalities, have never understood themselves in isolation from the civilizations around them.

KUKULKAN AND POSTCLASSIC LOWLAND ORIGINS

A stranger-king whose arrival in the northern Yucatán peninsula marked the resurgence of Postclassic Maya civilization, Kukulkan is described in colonial Yucatec sources as having traveled from the west to found the great city of Mayapan, in what is now the Mexican state of Yucatán. There, he became the main object of worship in a cult that was initially centered on Mayapan's main temple-pyramid. After political collapse prompted Mayapan's abandonment in the mid-fifteenth century, Kukulkan's followers relocated the cult just 28 km (17.5 miles) south to Maní, where it persisted into the colonial period.

In fact, it was the mythology of Kukulkan and not just the founder figure that arrived in the northern Maya lowlands from central Mexico. His name is the Yucatec translation of Quetzalcoatl, the Nahuatl name of a feathered serpent god whose origins can be traced back at least to the Early Classic period. Like Quetzalcoatl, Kukulkan is a mythical founder who guided his people from a period of uncertainty and chaos into prosperity before mysteriously disappearing. Yet the Maya account of Kukulkan differs from the central Mexican myth of Quetzalcoatl in several key aspects. Most notable are the stranger-king's foreignness and the peaceful nature of his final departure from the Maya region. These differences suggest that the Yucatec did not just borrow the

A Postclassic Maya painting of a rain-bringing feathered serpent. Madrid Codex (fol. 14).

mythology of the feathered serpent wholesale from the west. In creating the figure of Kukulkan, they adapted the imported tradition to the reality of the Postclassic and colonial northern Maya lowlands.

The legendary figure of Kukulkan may well have been based on historical reality. There are two primary manifestations of the central Mexican feathered serpent. One is the god of wind and rain known as Ehecatl Quetzalcoatl, who was involved in creation and venerated in a cult that had persisted at least since the Early Classic rise of Teotihuacan. Another figure known as Topiltzin Quetzalcoatl—onomastically and conceptually associated with the god but historically a distinct character—is described in Nahua sources as a legendary ruler of the Toltecs at their capital, Tula (see Introduction).

The Maya figure appears to have been an adaptation of this latter aspect of the feathered serpent, given that Kukulkan's introduction in the northern lowlands starting in the ninth century coincided with a wave of Toltec influence in the area. In fact, Topiltzin Quetzalcoatl's cultural importance among the Toltecs was so strong that his priests were treated as embodiments of the mythohistorical persona, and his name was attached to the highest-ranking religious office. Unfortunately, we do not know Kukulkan's full story as the Maya recorded it. Scholars' painstaking reconstruction of the surviving evidence, from fragmented alphabetic texts written during the colonial period and imagery recovered from archaeological sites, sketches a portrait of a mysterious foreigner whose advent marked an inflection point in the trajectory of Postclassic Yucatec society.

In fact, Kukulkan's story begins prior to his arrival in the northern lowlands with the establishment of the great Maya city of Chichen Itza. Its founders, known as the Itza', were newcomers who had arrived in the northern lowlands from the south long ago, perhaps during the Classic period. Unlike the northern lowlands' native Yucatec population, the Itza' spoke another Mayan tongue, likely Chontal, that rang crude and broken in the ears of locals.

Under the Itza's auspices, a grand new city was erected in the Maya lowlands, with stone walls, vaulted roofs, monumental sculptures, and broad causeways. Sometime after or, perhaps, in parallel with the Itza's arrival, a strange central Mexican ruler-priest appeared at Chichen Itza. Maya sources are silent on the precise origins of this interloper, whose Nahuatl name, Quetzalcoatl, they rendered in their language as Kukulkan. To Yucatec historians, the foreigner's identity was less important than the consequences of his presence in their homeland and of his assumption of power at Chichen Itza.

A mural in the Temple of the Warriors at Chichen Itza, Yucatán, Mexico, includes among various scenes of Postclassic Maya life a feathered serpent hovering over a roofed structure and its occupants (top right).

A Late Classic figurine from Aguateca, Petén, Guatemala, of a bearded nobleman wearing a tall headdress, beaded necklace with pendant, and large earspools.

When he appeared at Chichen Itza, Kukulkan was not alone. The commanding leader was accompanied by some twenty Toltec followers who, unlike the largely barefaced Maya peoples of the Yucatán, sported long beards. Their clothes were long, their feet covered in sandals, and their heads crowned with headdresses featuring a distinctive avian ornament that dangled over their foreheads. Whereas Maya soldiers tended to carry spears, knives, or axes, the warriors in Kukulkan's entourage carried central Mexican-style spear-throwers or *atlatls*. The Toltecs' bodies glittered as they moved, sunlight reflecting off the round mirrors of polished pyrite that they wore on their backs.

Kukulkan and his entourage brought with them precious goods made of metal and turquoise, unfamiliar materials—the latter was probably sourced in what is now the southwestern United States, thousands of kilometers northwest of the Yucatán peninsula—that elicited wonder and admiration among the Maya. The foreigners from the west also introduced a new cult of worship, with Kukulkan at its head. Kukulkan was himself a god of fevers, and his companions had their own supernatural specialties. The religious tradition required adherents to fast, present offerings, and conduct ritual performances as part of their worship. As high priest, Kukulkan set an example for his followers by living a chaste life without female companionship. For that reason, too, he did not have any children of his own.

It was in Kukulkan's honor that Chichen Itza's greatest pyramid was constructed. Referred to today as the Castillo ("castle"), the stepped pyramid with a staircase climbing up each of its four sides towered over the massive plaza. Perched at its peak, 24 m (79 ft) above ground, stood a quadrangular temple dedicated to Kukulkan, where priests performed sacrifices and other ceremonies for him. Balustrades along the pyramid's staircase featured the feathered serpent in honor of its namesake.

Chichen Itza's power grew under Kukulkan's guidance, as he quelled the political unrest and social instability that had begun to bubble up after the death of local Itza' rulers. Thanks to his strong leadership, Chichen Itza dominated the northern lowlands during the tenth and eleventh centuries. Political prominence brought economic wealth, too. The city received tribute from allies in Guatemala to the south, in Chiapas to the southwest, and in central Mexico to the far west, all of whom sought the favor and mercy of Kukulkan. Goods like honey, wildfowl, and woven cotton blankets flowed into the city, which could also count on its allies to furnish troops in times of war.

Although Chichen Itza flourished under him, the feathered serpent lord also oversaw the beginning of the end of the city's power in the eleventh century. It was Kukulkan, after all, who spurred the founding of the next great Postclassic city in the northern lowlands. He chose a patch of good land, some fifteen to twenty leagues inland from the Gulf Coast and about eight leagues south of Tiho, which in the colonial period would become the city of Mérida. The site was strategically advantageous and well-resourced, with over a dozen cenotes that could provide easy access to groundwater for a large urban population. There, the foreigner from the west and his followers agreed to create a new capital that would succeed Chichen Itza as the region's political and economic hub. They began to build a new city of stone, which they called Mayapan, "Banner (or Standard) of the Maya."

Kukulkan's Mayapan was ringed by an imposing wall that stretched over 9 km (5.5 miles) long, within which a population of tens of thousands took up residence. A ceremonial center lay at the city's heart, delineated by another, lower stone wall and accessible by just two gates. In this sanctuary, Kukulkan ordered the construction of many stone structures, including a round building and a series of colonnaded halls. The noble families of Mayapan settled into fine houses there, each representative having been awarded land and rulership over a nearby town according to his privilege.

Of all the impressive constructions at Mayapan, the grandest pyramid was dedicated to the feathered serpent founder. Although it stood a comparatively modest 15 m (49 ft) tall, it was modeled on the Castillo at Chichen Itza and, like that earlier building, featured four

Reconstructed view of Postclassic Chichen Itza, looking southward from the Sacred Cenote down the causeway to the ceremonial center. In the middle of the plaza sits the Castillo, with the temple of Kukulkan at its peak.

radial stairways ascending the steeply stepped sides. The high priests of the new pyramid's crowning temple, like the ruling Kukulkan himself, lived alongside the nobles within the walled sanctuary at the city center. Standing in the core of the ceremonial district, the pyramid of Kukulkan marked Mayapan's rise as the successor to Chichen Itza as the most powerful Postclassic center of power in the northern lowlands.

At Mayapan, too, Kukulkan's reign was marked by peace and prosperity. After several years, however, the priest-lord became restless and felt a desire to return to his homeland in the west. Finally, he decided to leave behind his subjects and companions to return to Mexico, leaving authority over Mayapan in the hands of the council of local nobles. On his journey westward, Kukulkan

The pyramid dedicated to Kukulkan rises above the ceremonial center of Mayapan, Yucatán, Mexico.

stopped to rest in Champotón, a town on the Gulf Coast of what is now Campeche. There, too, he constructed a modest pyramid on the shore as a testament to his visit.

When Kukulkan left the northern Yucatán peninsula, he did not merely return to central Mexico; he ascended into heaven to be with the other gods. Thus, for every year after his departure, during the month Xul, his followers celebrated a series of ceremonies for Kukulkan at Mayapan and, later, at Maní. Surrounding communities made an annual donation to Maní of extravagant banners woven from the feathers of tropical birds, in honor of the lord who had come to their ancestors from the west. During these ceremonies, Kukulkan came down to his people to receive their offerings and worship before returning to his place in the sky above.

STRANGER-KINGS AND FOREIGN FOUNDERS

Even if the myth of Topiltzin Quetzalcoatl was based on a historical person, the Toltecs who arrived at Chichen Itza bearing his name were more likely representatives of his cult rather than the original Topiltzin Quetzalcoatl himself. As a mythical founder, Kukulkan embodies Postclassic Yucatec culture's status as a product of both earlier Classic Maya civilization and of interactions with central Mexico, with which the Maya had been in contact for centuries. Unlike an origin myth, the story of Kukulkan does not account for the ethnogenesis of a distinct population. Instead, it provides historical context for sociopolitical developments—including the arrival of a new ruler and cult of worship and the transfer of power from one center to another—that Yucatec communities experienced in the generations prior to the arrival of Europeans in the early sixteenth century.

The next tale moves forward in time to precisely that moment of first encounter between the Maya and the Spanish. In contrast to the account of Kukulkan, this myth describes initial Indigenous resistance to the newcomers and details the devastation that the encounter brought to the region. Its protagonist is not a foreign founding figure, but a Maya warrior who lost his life defending against the foreign incursion. Much as in the story of Kukulkan, however, the arrival of a powerful stranger—in this case, Spanish conquistador Pedro de Alvarado—marks a clear break in Maya history that permanently altered the world inherited by the storytellers and their descendants.

The Battle of Pachaj, which took place in 1524 just outside of the modern-day town of Xela (Quetzaltenango), represents an inflection point in Maya and Guatemalan history. It is also an event whose historiographic interpretation confounds attempts to clearly distinguish myth from history (see Introduction). Surviving information about the confrontation, including the climatic duel between K'iche' leader Tekum Uman and Spanish conquistador Pedro de Alvarado, originates almost entirely from K'iche' sources. Spaniards who fought at Pachaj, including Alvarado and Bernal Díaz del Castillo, only describe the confrontation in passing, if they mention it at all; at most, they cast the battle as a minor episode in a years-long process of imperial conquest. Pictorial and written records from central Mexicans who fought in Alvarado's army similarly portray the battle as merely one among many in the region, without providing any additional details about it.

K'iche' accounts of the encounter between Tekum Uman and Alvarado were probably first written down in the mid- to late sixteenth century. By then, it was apparent that the colonial invaders intended to stay. In each source, the story of the battle is recorded as part of a longer land title claiming ancestral rights and privileges. Every version thus reflects the unique perspective of the K'iche' community that composed it. Collectively, these accounts do not so much contradict each other as provide complementary interpretations of the battle and its consequences. Moreover, Tekum Uman's personal biography and narrative representation suggest that the K'iche' authors who recorded his deeds considered him the portent of a later hero who would arise to finish the fallen fighter's work of expelling the foreign invaders.

The most detailed narrative of the Battle of Pachaj and the duel between Tekum Uman and Alvarado covers the last several pages of a document known today as the *Title of Nija'ib' I* or the *Title of*

Quetzaltenango and Momostenango. It was composed by members of the Nija'ib' division of the Nima K'iche', one of the four major K'iche' amaq's at Q'umarkaaj. Another retelling is found in the *Title of Ajpop Huitzitzil Tz'unun*, whose authors were K'iche' lords from Quetzaltenango and Santa Cruz del Quiché. Both documents were presumably written first in K'iche', although only Spanish translations have survived.

The *Title of K'oyoy*, which bears the signature of the same scribe as the *Title of Ajpop Huitzitzil Tz'unun*, offers a third perspective on the Battle of Pachaj. Composed by members of the K'oyoy Saqorowach lineage at Q'umarkaaj, this text is unique in being the only known K'iche'-language account of the conflict from the sixteenth century. Unfortunately, however, the section about the battle is relatively short and badly damaged. A fourth document, the *Title of Xecul* or *Ajpop Quejam*, is mentioned by seventeenth-century Guatemalan chronicler Francisco Antonio de Fuentes y Guzmán, a descendant of conquistador Díaz del Castillo, but its whereabouts today are unknown.

The hero of the Battle of Pachaj, the sixteenth-century K'iche' warrior Tekum Uman who faced off against Alvarado, is perhaps the most famous Indigenous figure in Guatemala's historical memory today. He has been a legend among the K'iche' and other highland groups for centuries, and since the end of the colonial period in the early nineteenth century, he has been elevated to a symbol of Guatemalan national pride. The sixteenth-century warrior's illustrious reputation, molded by assumptions about the sources from which scholars have reconstructed his biography, have cast his life and death much in the same terms as other mythic Maya heroes.

Tekum Uman and the Battle of Pachaj

In early 1524, conquistador Pedro de Alvarado led several thousand Indigenous allies and a few hundred Spanish compatriots on the first Spanish-led invasion of modern-day Guatemala. After an initial, hard-fought victory at Xetulul, a settlement on Guatemala's Pacific coast, Alvarado directed his troops eastward and upward into the highlands. Moving in from the coast, they pushed deeper into K'iche' territory through rough terrain that was difficult to traverse even on horseback.

Meanwhile, survivors of the battle at Xetulul sent messengers to warn the residents of Xelajuj Kej, Sapoqlaj, Q'umarkaaj, and other highland K'iche' towns about the advancing invaders. In response, the Maya communities began arming themselves, constructing defensive walls and excavating deep pits that they lined with spears and camouflaged to trap unsuspecting cavalry.

Having received word of the foreign incursion, the K'iche' lord at Q'umarkaaj summoned his best captain, Tekum Uman, the grandson of the legendary Postclassic warrior K'iq'ab', to confront the invading army. Tekum Uman assembled his army from surrounding K'iche' towns in the mountains near Chwi' Miq'ina'. Numbering in the thousands, the soldiers represented all the major K'iche' towns and lineages.

Before departing with his troops, Tekum Uman put on the insignias appropriate to his rank as a decorated K'iche' warrior, fixing polished mirrors to his forehead and back and donning a headdress glittering with jewels. He also wore feathered wings on his arms and legs that allowed him to take flight as an eagle. The imposing captain and his soldiers were sent off with music and dance in the streets. Dozens of standard-bearers, waving banners luxuriously decorated

The *Lienzo de Quauhquechollan*

The pictorial document now known as the *Lienzo de Quauhquechollan* was painted on cloth by Nahuas from the town for which it is named, now San Martín Huaquechula in the Mexican state of Puebla. The early sixteenth-century cloth documents the Quauhquecholtecas' service alongside the Spanish in the second wave of invasion into Guatemala led by Jorge de Alvarado, Pedro's younger brother. Most battles portrayed on the lienzo occurred between 1527 and 1529 in Mexico and Guatemala, making it an invaluable source of information on the first generation of the Spanish conquest from the perspective of some of its Indigenous protagonists.

A representation of fighting in Kaqchikel territory in 1527 from the *Lienzo de Quauhquechollan*, c. 1530. Note the Quauhquecholteca warrior dressed as an eagle, the defensive barriers across roads, and the spear pit into which another Quauhquecholteca has fallen.

with precious stones and metals above their heads, led the army on its march to confront the foreign intruders.

After crossing the coastal piedmont into the highlands, Alvarado and his men made a month-long stopover to rest and regroup at the

A flutist and a drummer (center) make music in front of a third person, possibly a dancer (right), in a scene from a colonial-period mural in the Ixil town of Chajul, El Quiché, Guatemala.

foot of the volcano Xelajuj No'j, near Xelajuj Kej. During the same period, another force of several thousand K'iche' troops converged at Chwa Ab'aj, where they constructed a series of stone walls and ditches to thwart the invaders. For several weeks, they were able to impede Alvarado's outnumbered forces, holding them at a stalemate. Finally, in mid-February 1524, the confrontation came to a head just outside Xelajuj No'j at Pachaj, to which the Spaniards later referred as El Pinal.

A K'iche' captain, outfitted as an eagle, led several thousand soldiers in a midnight attack from the town of Xepach, less than two kilometers from the base of Xelajuj No'j. Their goal was to kill Alvarado, but they were stymied by the appearance of a young girl, either white-skinned or dressed in white, who blocked their entrance into Alvarado's camp. The K'iche' soldiers tried to attack her, but they fell to the ground. They saw that she was being defended by strange, footless birds, which blinded the attackers. The K'iche' soldiers, confused and unable to see, had to abandon the mission and retreat to their base.

After the other K'iche' commanders heard about the confrontation with the girl surrounded by birds, they sent another captain, don Francisco Iskin Nija'ib', to lead a second charge against Alvarado. His men, too, were stopped on the battlefield, this time by a white dove hovering above and defending the invading troops. Each time the K'iche' troops picked themselves up off the ground and rallied to charge again, they were blinded. The Nija'ib' captain was eventually forced to retreat. He sent a message to the K'iche' leadership at Q'umarkaaj, some 40 km (25 miles) to the northeast, reporting on the failed attacks and the strange birds and young girl who had impeded them.

Alvarado, meanwhile, was coordinating his own maneuvers. Under his direction, a contingent of Spanish and Tlaxcaltec soldiers from central Mexico ambushed the K'iche' settlement of Chwa Raal, east of Xelajuj Kej, where they killed hundreds of residents with their firearms, lances, crossbows, spades, daggers, and swords. They bound, tortured, and interrogated survivors to coerce them into revealing where they had hidden the gold that the Spaniards were obsessively seeking. To put an end to their suffering, the people of Chwa Raal eventually capitulated. Two local K'iche' captains—both accomplished warriors who manifested as an eagle and a cougar, respectively—handed over precious stones and metals to the invaders, in addition to arranging food and shelter for them.

By this point, Tekum Uman and his troops had marched the 20 km (12.5 miles) southwest from Chwi' Miq'ina', armed with bows, arrows, slings, spears, and clubs studded with obsidian blades. They were received on the outskirts of Xelajuj Kej with fanfare similar to what had accompanied their send-off. But the festive atmosphere did not last. The famous captain, angered by the Spanish attack on Chwa Raal, sent a challenge to the invaders.

In response to Tekum Uman's challenge, Alvarado marched with thousands of Indigenous allies, plus a few hundred Spaniards, to meet the K'iche' captain and his army on the plains near Pachaj. There, the conquistador offered to make peace with the K'iche', in return for their submission to the Spanish crown. Tekum Uman refused, saying that he preferred to see the invaders demonstrate their strength on the battlefield.

Over the next several hours of fighting, some of Alvarado's men fell, but the K'iche' suffered especially heavy losses. Neither side gained much ground. To turn the tide, Tekum Uman, richly attired as an eagle and sparkling with a crown of gold, a crown of pearls,

High-ranking Late Classic Maya warriors—many wearing animal headdresses—present captives to king Yajaw Chan Muwaan of Bonampak (top center), shortly after a battle that likely took place on 19 July 786. Wall mural from Bonampak, Chiapas, Mexico.

and a crown of diamonds and emeralds, took flight toward Alvarado. He was unable to approach the Spaniard on his first attack. On the second, he came close enough to thrust his spear at the conquistador. But the blade missed its intended target. Instead, it hit Alvarado's horse and sliced off the animal's head.

Tekum Uman rose in flight once again to make a third attempt. This time, Alvarado was waiting in anticipation of another offensive. He met the K'iche' captain with his own metal blade, piercing the decorated soldier through the torso.

The fatal blow brought Tekum Uman to the ground. Two hairless dogs approached his body and began to scavenge, but Alvarado stopped them. The conquistador was amazed by Tekum Uman's three crowns luxuriously inlaid with precious stones and by his colorful feathers from the quetzal and other tropical birds. He was so impressed by the fallen warrior that he called over his troops to admire his commanding opponent. He told them that he had never seen such a gallant captain, not even during his prior conquests in Mexico. To commemorate the magnificent soldier, Alvarado conferred upon the nearby town of Xelajuj Kej the name Quetzaltenango, or "Walled Place of the Quetzal Bird" in Nahuatl, the language of many of his central Mexican allies.

The remaining K'iche' forces, seeing that their captain had been vanquished, retreated to the surrounding hills as Alvarado's troops gave chase. So many compatriots had fallen that the sun turned red in the sky, and their blood flowed in a river through the landscape. In memory of the bloodshed, the K'iche' later referred to the nearby town as Kik'el (K'iche' "Blood," now the town of Olintepeque).

At the end of the day, Alvarado and his army returned from their victory to the newly renamed town of Quetzaltenango for food and rest. They were met by a cohort of K'iche' lords from major towns in the region, who acknowledged the conquistador's victory. They also agreed to be baptized by the two Dominican friars and two Franciscan friars who had accompanied Alvarado's party to Guatemala. To mark the nobles' status as subjects of the Spanish Crown and Christians, Alvarado bestowed upon them the title of *don*, "Sir." He awarded each one a sword and Spanish-style clothing, both privileges that were not available to most Indigenous persons in colonial society.

Nahuatl Toponyms in Guatemala

Now the capital of the Guatemalan Department of Totonicapán, San Miguel Totonicapán was an important K'iche' center known as Chuwi' Miq'ina' ("Above the Hot Water"). Like so many other towns in the Guatemalan highlands, it was renamed during the colonial period using the Nahuatl translation of the Maya toponym.

When Pedro de Alvarado arrived in Guatemala in 1524, he was accompanied by a few hundred Spaniards. Most of his army, however, consisted of Indigenous soldiers from central Mexico and Oaxaca. Among them were many from the central Mexican city-state Tlaxcala, who had joined forces with the Spaniards to conquer their sworn rivals, the Aztecs. When the Spaniards arrived in Guatemala, their Tlaxcalan allies referred to the places they encountered in their own language, Nahuatl. The Spanish colonial administration adopted the Nahuatl translations for many Mayan-language place names. The toponyms are still found across the landscape of modern-day Guatemala and include Totonicapán, Mazatenango (from K'iche' K'aqol Kej, "Deer Hunter"), Chimaltenango (from Kaqchikel B'oko', "Shield"), Zapotitlán (from K'iche' Xetulul, "Below the Zapote Tree"), and Chichicastenango (from K'iche' Chuwila', "Above the Nettles"), among others.

Starting in 1972, the Guatemalan banknote for a half-quetzal or fifty cents featured a portrait of Tekum Uman on the obverse. The banknote was gradually phased out in the late 1990s in favor of a coin of equal value.

The newly baptized K'iche' noblemen were also christened with Spanish personal and family names, which were often inspired by a conquistador. Thus, after the Battle of Pachaj and their baptism, the Indigenous lords became known as José Cardenas, Pedro Lucas Cardenas, Andrés de Chávez, Juan Osorio Cortés, Francisco Cardenas Hernández, Martín Mejía, Diego Pérez, Pedro Alvarado Ramírez, Jorge Solís, Andrés Vásquez, Martín Velásquez, Francisco Vico, Tomás Vitoria, and Bartolomé López Vitorio. The K'iche' noblemen thanked Alvarado for reaffirming their authority within the new colonial order by bringing him precious stones, pearls, and gold. Finally, they called back their people who had fled to the hills to escape the fighting. They brought the refugees back to the conquistador and his clergymen so that they could all be baptized as subjects of the new Catholic religion and of the Spanish Crown.

Tekum Uman in Guatemalan Mythohistory

The contours of this story are historically uncontested, including the basic makeup of the invading troops, the location and timing of the first battles with the K'iche', and the encounters' consequences for local political history. Other features of the K'iche' accounts, however, challenge literal interpretation. In response, scholars have questioned whether Tekum Uman was a historical protagonist or a mythical figure invented after the fact to explain the success of the Spanish conquest.

Certainly, some aspects of the K'iche' narratives of the Battle of Pachaj are empirically improbable. No Spanish source attests to the presence of priests in Alvarado's expedition party that departed Tenochtitlan for Guatemala in 1523. Although Maya accounts of initial encounters with the Spanish often associate military conquest with baptism, the two events were rarely chronologically correlated

Alvarado's purported signature at the end of the *Title of Quetzaltenango and Momostenango* (fol. 22r).

in practice. Dominican and Franciscan friars would not arrive in Guatemala until more than a decade later. In addition, the oversized signature at the end of the lengthiest record of the battle, the *Title of Quetzaltenango and Momostenango*, is almost certainly not that of the restless Alvarado. The infamously brutal conquistador devoted his remaining life to conquest and would not have cared to stick around to supervise the baptism of his subjugated foes.

The lists of noblemen whom Spanish friars baptized after the K'iche' surrender at Pachaj, under Alvarado's supervision, also vary by source. The individuals cited here include all those whose full personal and family names are indicated in at least one of the three colonial-period sources. Each document lists between six to eleven persons, with little overlap between them. Only Juan Osorio Cortés, Andrés de Chávez, and Martín Mejía are named in two texts, and no one appears in all three. What the lists do have in common, however, is that they consistently prioritize figures directly connected to the community where the document was penned. The respective authors ensured that their ancestors were identified among the select few baptized by the priests and honored with gifts from Alvarado himself.

Much doubt about Tekum Uman's existence is based on negative evidence—in other words, on the K'iche' hero's absence from reports by Spanish conquistadors. Alvarado does not cite any Indigenous leader by name in his report to Cortés dated 11 April 1524, which included his account of the conquest of Quetzaltenango. He only suggests that the opponents killed in that confrontation included many "captains and lords and distinguished persons." More tellingly, Díaz del Castillo, a Spaniard best known for his lengthy chronicle of exploits during the conquest, notes in a brief description of the battle of Quetzaltenango that "many soldiers were wounded as well

Scene 77 of the *Lienzo de Tlaxcala* illustrates K'iche' warriors confronting Spanish and Tlaxcalan invaders at Xela (Quetzaltenango), *c.* 1552.

as a horse, and it seems that some Indian Chieftains from that pueblo itself were killed, as well as from all that country, so that after the victory those pueblos had a great fear of Alvarado, and the whole of the district agreed to send to him and beg for peace." Tekum Uman may well have been one of these fallen "chieftains." Even if he was not, it would not be surprising if either Spaniard omitted, forgot, or never bothered to learn the name of a defeated Indigenous captain.

Doubts about the historicity of Tekum Uman's person and deeds are based on a Spanish-centric perspective of the invasion of Guatemala. There is no reason to question the K'iche' sources' veracity. They offer different details on the event, but do not contradict each other in any meaningful way. Cultural and historical context support a relatively literal reading of the narrative of the Battle of Pachaj, including its apparently supernatural aspects. Historians have proposed that the young girl dressed in white who was surrounded by footless birds that blinded the attackers is a description of a banner depicting the Virgin Mary surrounded by cherubs, which to those unfamiliar with Catholic imagery do resemble supernatural birds, given their child-like features and wings. Even if the Spaniards did not carry such an image with them into battle at Pachaj, the reference to the mother of Jesus and her heavenly companions may have been inserted retroactively. Writing a generation or two later with the benefit of hindsight and greater knowledge of Catholicism, the K'iche' authors could have used this motif to represent the Spaniards' claim that their God had led them to victory and to explain their own ancestors' ill-fated attempts to stop the foreign invaders.

Indigenous sources also claim that Tekum Uman "put on wings with which he flew" to meet Alvarado and his army in combat. The captain followed standard practice for elite central Mexican and highland Maya warriors in going into battle as a fierce animal, usually a jaguar or an eagle. The *Lienzo de Quauhquechollan* and other Mesoamerican pictorial sources illustrate Indigenous soldiers as eagles or jaguars. For Tekum Uman and his compatriots, his avian presentation was no mere costume; it embodied his status as a *nawal* and his fierceness and prowess as a combatant.

Even Tekum Uman's eagle nawal attacking from the air could not down Alvarado, much as the highland Maya could not avert the imposition of Spanish colonialism. K'iche' accounts of the violent encounter at Pachaj were penned just a few decades later, in the mid- to late sixteenth century. By then, Q'umarkaaj was an overgrown landscape of blackened ruins, and the Kaqchikel and Tz'utujil had, like the K'iche', long surrendered to the Spanish. Even Alvarado himself had died, crushed by his horse in the Mixtón War while fighting against the Caxcanes and their allies in northwestern Mexico.

Nonetheless, comparison with other accounts of Maya heroes suggests a more optimistic reading of Tekum Uman's demise. When the *Popol Vuh* was first written down in alphabetic form, the Hero Twins' primordial deeds lay so far in the past that the authors could clearly perceive their place in the longer arc of K'iche' history.

A Classic Maya stucco sculpture recovered near Lake Petén Itzá, Guatemala, shows a crouching man, perhaps a warrior, clad in a jaguar mask and skirt.

The *Nawal*

A *nawal* (sometimes written *nahual* or *nagual*) is a powerful, supernatural being that could shape-shift between human and animal form. The term is derived from Nahuatl *nahual*, meaning "transform, convert, disguise, trick," and refers to a phenomenon found across Indigenous Mesoamerica, although the characteristics ascribed to nawals varies by local tradition. Although the origins of the Mesoamerican nawal are unknown, the earliest evidence comes from Classic Maya hieroglyphic texts, where the beings are mentioned by the fifth century, and imagery painted on ceramic vessels, where they appear as hybrid creatures with a mixture of animal, human, and divine features.

With the hindsight of many generations, they interpreted the Hero Twins' failings, culminating in their execution, as stumbles along a path to ultimate triumph. If anything, the early setbacks only made the boys' comeback all the more improbable, elevating their heroic status.

In the K'iche' telling of the Battle of Pachaj, the immediate consequences of Tekum Uman's death are Christianization and Spanish colonialism. The authors, themselves only a few years removed from the battle, give no indication of how they might perceive their hero's legacy and deeds in the long term. Did they perhaps hope, or even expect, that a successor to Tekum Uman would eventually emerge to lead a K'iche' rebellion against the foreign invaders? From this perspective, Tekum Uman's demise at Pachaj does not represent a permanent loss of Maya autonomy. Instead, it paves the way for the rise of a future hero with the cleverness and means to avenge the fallen Postclassic warrior.

EPILOGUE

Maya peoples have experienced profound changes in the five hundred years since Pedro de Alvarado and his troops first entered highland Guatemala. The short-term consequences of Spanish colonialism included population collapse, political and economic reorganization, and evangelization. Rural Indigenous communities were forcibly resettled or "congregated" into Spanish-style towns for easier administration, religion conversion, and control. Maya leaders were tasked with ensuring that their communities fulfilled the Spanish Crown's burdensome tribute demands. Missionaries suppressed Indigenous religious practices and demanded at least superficial acceptance of and participation in Catholicism. They confiscated Postclassic documents and proscribed use of the hieroglyphic script, replacing it with modified versions of their own Roman alphabet.

For the last half-millennium, most Maya peoples have practiced a hybrid form of Catholicism that emerged during the encounter with Indigenous religious practices. An influx of Protestant missionaries since the mid-twentieth century has resulted in a rapid proliferation of other forms of Christianity in the region. As society and the economy have become more globalized, more Maya persons are immigrating or traveling internationally, especially to North America. They are drawing on modern technologies to create new outlets of cultural expression that range from digital artwork and popular music to social media.

At the same time, the world has become more curious about the Maya. During the colonial period, Catholic missionaries meticulously documented Mayan languages and Maya culture; their primary goal was not to preserve or valorize Indigenous knowledge, however, but to displace it. Since European and North American explorers began publishing illustrated accounts of their travels in the early nineteenth century, the Maya region has become a source of global fascination for its own sake. Popularization of academic archaeology has fed growing public interest in a process accelerated by the rise of television, public-facing periodicals like *National Geographic*, and digital media. Tourism has become a major industry in the Maya region, and archaeological sites represent key attractions in northern Guatemala and the Yucatán peninsula in particular. In academia, Maya studies has become an established field that is taught and learned in anthropology, art history, archaeology, history, linguistics, and area studies courses at universities across North and Central America and Europe.

These developments have significantly expanded access to the myths that the Maya have told about themselves. None of the stories recounted in this volume was widely known or disseminated outside of the Maya region before the nineteenth century. Major advances in decipherment have made it possible for epigraphers, or experts in hieroglyphic writing, to read texts that the pre-colonial Maya recorded on ceramic and stone. Colonial manuscripts in local, national, and international archives document Maya narratives that were dictated onto paper. Generations of ethnographers have recorded hundreds of tales from storytellers across the region, representing every Mayan language still spoken today.

The same dynamic has led to a boom in stories that scholars, most of whom have historically been non-Maya, tell about the Maya. Archaeologists and historians have reconstructed increasingly detailed histories based on material remains, textual sources, and oral histories. Linguists have produced more precise documentation of contemporary Mayan languages, as well as historical reconstructions of languages that are no longer spoken. Art historians can now interpret ancient images whose density and cultural specificity long stymied modern viewers. Anthropologists' attentive observations in Maya communities have generated insights into ritual practice, economic activity, language use, gender, ethnicity, and other aspects of society and culture. The result is a richer, more nuanced understanding of the past and present of Maya peoples.

At the same time, increased interest in and access to information about the Maya has fueled misconceptions and even malicious appropriations of their histories. Global obsession with the impending "Maya apocalypse" in 2012 was based on a misinterpretation of the Maya calendar's cyclical nature, and public intellectuals' attempts to set the record straight barely broke through the doomsday clamor. Members of the Church of Jesus Christ of Latter-day Saints continue to search for evidence linking ancient Maya civilization with foundational events in the Book of Mormon. Pseudo-archaeological theories propagated by figures like Erich von Däniken claim that Classic Maya civilization was influenced, if not built, by extraterrestrials. These myths about the Maya are often sold as entertainment, but they reinforce xenophobic and racist narratives by suggesting that Indigenous peoples could not have created such sophisticated civilizations without outside intervention. (Similar conspiracy theories about aliens constructing the Greek Parthenon or the Vikings being a lost tribe of Israel have had far less popular uptake.)

The myths of the Maya reflect ongoing adaptation to a changing world. As they have for millennia, Maya peoples will continue to adapt their histories to account for an evolving understanding of the past and its relationship to the present and future. Much in the same way, academics, popular enthusiasts, and pseudo-scientists will continue to tell their own stories about the Maya. Myths of and about the Maya will interact with each other, too, in unpredictable and probably surprising ways. We all have a choice about the narratives that we engage with, share, and create. In the end, the stories that we tell about other people—people separated from us by time, culture, gender, ethnicity, among other markers of identity—say more about ourselves than about the stories' ostensible subjects.

FURTHER READING

There is an overwhelming abundance of literature about Maya myths and civilization; for those interested in learning more, below are some suggestions to get started. The reading list for each chapter includes the sources from which the myths were compiled, plus additional publications that informed interpretation of the myths. The "Other References" list offers a wider range of readings about Maya history, including those consulted in composing the Introduction and box texts. Some are primary sources, but most are secondary literature representing the disciplines of archaeology, anthropology, art history, ethnohistory, epigraphy, linguistics, and religious studies.

Some publications are quite dense and specialized, and will be most useful to those with some background in Maya studies. For those seeking a general overview, the volumes by Houston and Inomata (2009) and Martin and Grube (2008) are accessible, well-written introductions to Classic Maya civilization, and Chinchilla Mazariegos (2017) provides a richly illustrated guide to Classic Maya religion and mythology. Those interested in the colonial era will enjoy the Restall and Asselbergs (2007) edition of conquest accounts, and Christenson (2007, 2022), Edmonson (1986), and Maxwell and Hill (2006) provide well-informed, fluent English translations of four important colonial-period Maya sources.

CHAPTER 1

Translation of quotation in "The Creation of the *Winals*" on p. 30, taken from Knowlton 2010, p. 156. Translations of quotations in "Broken Pots and Wild Beasts" on pp. 43–44, 46, taken from Christenson 2007, pp. 87–88. Translations of quotations in "A Rabbit Robs the Lord of the Underworld" on pp. 52, 54, taken from Beliaev and Davletshin 2006, p. 38, and Bernal Romero 2014, pp. 31 and 35.

Beliaev, Dmitri, and Albert Davletshin. 2006. "Los sujetos novelísticos y las palabras obscenas: los mitos, los cuentos y las anécdotas en los textos mayas sobre la cerámica del Período Clásico." In *Sacred Books, Sacred Languages: Two Thousand Years of Ritual and Religious Maya Literature*, Rogelio Valencia Rivera and Geneviève Le Fort (eds), pp. 21–44. Anton Saurwein, Markt Schwaben.

Bernal Romero, Guillermo. 2014. *El dios viejo y el conejo: un mito maya contado en las inscripciones jeroglíficas*. Resistencia, México.

Christenson, Allen J. 2007. *Popol Vuh: The Sacred Book of the Maya*. University of Oklahoma Press, Norman, OK.

Edmonson, Munro S. 1986. *Heaven Born Merida and its Destiny: The Book of Chilam Balam of Chumayel*. University of Texas Press, Austin, TX.

Knowlton, Timothy W. 2010. *Maya Creation Myths: Words and Worlds of the Chilam Balam*. University Press of Colorado, Boulder, CO.

Maxwell, Judith M., and Robert M. Hill. 2006. *Kaqchikel Chronicles: The Definitive Edition*. University of Texas Press, Austin, TX.

CHAPTER 2

Translations of quotations from "A Blowgunner and a Bird" on pp. 61, 62, 63, taken from Christenson 2007, pp. 98–99. Translation of quotations from "Blue Sun" on pp. 67, 68, 69, 71–74 taken from Slocum 1965, pp. 9–16; Translation of quotations from Tsotsil version on p. 72, taken from Gossen 2002, pp. 277, 283. Translations of quotations from "A Heavenly Triangle" p. 80 taken from Thompson 1930, p. 131.

Braakhuis, H.E.M. 1987. "Sun's Voyage to the City of the Vultures: A Classic Mayan Funerary Theme." *Zeitschrift für Ethnologie* 112(2): 237–60.

Cruz Torres, Mario Enrique de la. 1965. *Rubelpec: Cuentos y leyendas de Senahú, Alta Verapaz.* Colección Contemporáneos 83. Departamento Editorial "José de Pineda Ibarra," Ministerio de Educación, Guatemala.

Gossen, Gary H. (ed.). 2002. *Four Creations: An Epic Story of the Chiapas Mayas.* University of Oklahoma Press, Norman, OK.

Hopkins, Nicholas A., J. Kathryn Josserand, and Ausencio Cruz Guzmán. 2016. *Chol (Mayan) Folktales: A Collection of Stories from the Modern Maya of Southern Mexico.* University Press of Colorado, Boulder, CO.

Slocum, Marianna C. 1965. "The Origin of Corn and Other Tzeltal Myths." *Tlalocan* 5(1): 1–45.

Thompson, J. Eric S. 1930. Ethnology of the Mayas of Southern and Central British Honduras. *Anthropological Series* 17:25–213. Field Museum of Natural History, Publication 274.

Thompson, J. Eric S. 1970. *Maya History and Religion.* University of Oklahoma Press, Norman, OK.

CHAPTER 3

Braakhuis, H.E.M., and Kerry Hull. 2014. "Pluvial Aspects of the Mesoamerican Culture Hero: The 'Kumix Angel' of the Ch'orti' Mayas and Other Rain-Bringing Heroes." *Anthropos* 109(2): 449–66.

Fought, John. 1989. "Kumix: The Chorti Hero." In *General and Amerindian Ethnolinguistics*, Mary Ritchie Key and Henry M. Hoenigswald (eds), pp. 461–68. De Gruyter Mouton, Berlin.

Girard, Rafael. 1966. *Los mayas: su civilización, su historia, sus vinculaciones continentales.* Libro Mex, México.

Hull, Kerry M. 2009. "The Grand Ch'orti' Epic: The Story of the Kumix Angel." In *The Maya and their Sacred Narratives: Text and Context in Maya Mythologies: Proceedings of the 12th European Maya Conference, Geneva, December 7–8, 2007*, Geneviève Le Fort, Raphaël Gardiol, Sebastian Matteo, and Christophe Helmke (eds), pp. 131–40. Anton Saurwein, Markt Schwaben.

López García, Julián. 2010. *Kumix: la lluvia en la mitología maya – ch'orti'.* Ed. Cholsamaj, Guatemala.

Pérez Martínez, Vitalino (ed.). 1996. *Leyenda maya ch'orti'.* Proyecto Lingüístico Francisco Marroquin, Guatemala.

CHAPTER 4

Translations of quotations from "The Deal with the Weeds" on pp. 146, 147, taken from Gossen 2002, pp. 317–19.

Gossen, Gary H. (ed.). 2002. *Four Creations: An Epic Story of the Chiapas Mayas.* University of Oklahoma Press, Norman, OK.

Miles, Suzanne Whitelaw. 1960. "Mam Residence and the Maize Myth." In *Culture in History: Essays in Honor of Paul Radin*, Stanley Diamond (ed.), pp. 430–36. Columbia University Press, New York, NY.

Mondloch, James, Miguel Guarchaj Ch'o'x, and Diego Guarchaj. 1968. "Oral History #077: When the Food Rejected the People." K'iche' Maya Oral History Project, The University of New Mexico Digital Repository, https://digitalrepository.unm.edu/laii_kichemaya/63, accessed 23 October 2024.

Oakes, Maud. 1951. *The Two Crosses of Todos Santos: Survivals of Mayan Religious Ritual.* Princeton University Press, Princeton, NJ.

Quenon, Michel, and Geneviève Le Fort. 1997. "Rebirth and Resurrection in Maize God Iconography." In *The Maya Vase Book: A Corpus of Rollout Photographs of Maya Vases*, vol. 5, Barbara Kerr and Justin Kerr (eds), pp. 884–902. Kerr Associates, New York, NY.

Valladares, León A. 1957. *El hombre y el maíz: etnografía y etnopsicología de Colotenango.* Licenciatura thesis, Facultad de Humanidades, Universidad de San Carlos de Guatemala, Guatemala.

Wagley, Charles. 1941. *Economics of a Guatemalan Village.* The American Anthropological Association, Menasha.

CHAPTER 5

Translation of quotation from the *Xajil Chronicle* on p. 156, taken from Maxwell and Hill 2006, p. 23. Translations of quotations from "The Origins of the *Hach Winik*" on pp. 169, 172, taken from Boremanse 1984, p. 230. Translation of quotation from "Trophy Wife" on p. 170, taken from Boremanse 1986, p. 378. Translations of quotations from "The Origins of the *Hach Winik*" on pp. 171, 176 taken from Boremanse 1986, pp. 243, 245.

Boremanse, Didier. 1984. "Mitología y organización social entre los 'lacandones' (*hach winik*) de la selva chiapaneca." *Estudios de Cultura Maya* 15: 225–49.

Boremanse, Didier. 1986. *Contes et mythologie des indiens lacandons. Contribution à l'étude de la tradition orale maya.* Editions L'Harmattan, Paris.

Boremanse, Didier. 1998. *Hach Winik: The Lacandon Maya of Chiapas, Southern Mexico.* Institute for Mesoamerican Studies, Albany.

Christenson, Allen J. 2022. *The Title of Totonicapán.* University Press of Colorado, Louisville, CO.

Maxwell, Judith M., and Robert M. Hill. 2006. *Kaqchikel Chronicles: The Definitive Edition.* University of Texas Press, Austin, TX.

CHAPTER 6

Translation of quotation from Alvarado's letter to Cortés on p. 201 from Alvarado 1944, p. 388. Translation of quotation from Díaz del Castillo's conquest account on pp. 201–2 from Davíd Carrasco (Díaz del Castillo 2008), p. 232. Translation of quotation from the *Title of Quetzaltenango and Momostenango* on p. 203 from Matsumoto 2017, p. 364.

Alvarado, Pedro de. 1944. "Dos cartas de Pedro de Alvarado a Hernán Cortés." *Anales de la Sociedad de Geografía e Historia de Guatemala* 19(5): 386–96.

Carmack, Robert M., and James L. Mondloch. 2009. "Título K'oyoi." In *Crónicas Mesoamericanas (Tomo II)*, Horacio Cabezas Carcache (ed.), pp. 15–67. Universidad Mesoamericana, Guatemala.

Cortés, Hernán. 1946. *Cartas y relaciones, con otros documentos relativos a la vida y a las empresas del conquistador*. Ed. Nicolás Coronado. Emecé Editores, Buenos Aires.

Díaz del Castillo, Bernal. 2008. *The History of the Conquest of New Spain*. Trans. Davíd Carrasco. University of New Mexico Press, Albuquerque.

Folan, William J., David D. Bolles, and Jerald D. Ek. 2016. "On the Trail of Quetzalcoatl/Kukulcan: Tracing Mythic Interaction Routes and Networks in the Maya Lowlands." *Ancient Mesoamerica* 27(2): 293–318.

Gall, Francis. 1963. *Título del Ajpop Huitzitzil Tzunún [y] Probanza de méritos de los de León y Cardona*. Centro Editorial "José de Pineda Ibarra," Ministerio de Educación Pública, Guatemala.

Landa, Diego de. 1941 [1566]. *Landa's Relación de las cosas de Yucatán*. Trans. and ed. Alfred M. Tozzer. Peabody Museum, Cambridge, MA.

Las Casas, Bartolomé de. 1967. *Apologética historia sumaria*. Ed. Edmundo O'Gorman. Universidad Nacional Autónoma de México, Instituto de Investigaciones Históricas, México.

Matsumoto, Mallory E. 2017. *Land, Politics, and Memory in Five Nija'ib' K'iche' Títulos: "The Title and Proof of Our Ancestors"*. University Press of Colorado, Boulder, CO.

Nicholson, Henry B. 2001. *Topiltzin Quetzalcoatl: The Once and Future Lord of the Toltecs*. University of Colorado Press, Boulder, CO.

Recinos, Adrián. 1957. *Crónicas indígenas de Guatemala*. Editorial Universitaria de la Universidad de San Carlos de Guatemala, Guatemala.

OTHER REFERENCES

Carmack, Robert M. 2001. *Kik'ulmatajem le K'iche'aab'. Evolución del Reino K'iche'*. Cholsamaj, Guatemala.

Chinchilla Mazariegos, Oswaldo F. 2010. "La vagina dentada: una interpretación de la Estela 25 de Izapa y las guacamayas del juego de pelota de Copán." *Estudios de Cultura Maya* 36: 117–44.

Chinchilla Mazariegos, Oswaldo F. 2013. "Tecum, the Fallen Sun: Mesoamerican Cosmogony and the Spanish Conquest of Guatemala." *Ethnohistory* 60(4): 693–719.

Chinchilla Mazariegos, Oswaldo F. 2017. *Art and Myth of the Ancient Maya*. Yale University Press, New Haven, CT.

Christenson, Allen J. 2006. "You Are What You Speak: Maya as the Language of Maize." In *Maya Ethnicity: The Construction of Ethnic Identity from Preclassic to Modern Times*, Frauke Sachse (ed.), pp. 209–16. Anton Saurwein, Markt Schwaben.

Christenson, Allen J. 2010. "Maize Was Their Flesh: Ritual Feasting in the Maya Highlands." In *Pre-Columbian Foodways: Interdisciplinary Approaches to Food, Culture, and Markets in Ancient Mesoamerica*, John E. Staller and Michael D. Carrasco (eds), pp. 577–600. Springer, New York, NY.

Grube, Nikolai, and Werner Nahm. 1994. "A Census of Xibalba: A Complete Inventory of Way Characters on Maya Ceramics." In *The Maya Vase Book: A Corpus of Rollout Photographs of Maya Vases*, Vol. 4, Barbara Kerr and Justin Kerr (eds), pp. 686–715. Kerr Associates, New York, NY.

Houston, Stephen D., David Stuart and Karl A. Taube. 2006. *The Memory of Bones: Body, Being, and Experience among the Classic Maya*. University of Texas Press, Austin, TX.

Houston, Stephen D., and Takeshi Inomata. 2009. *The Classic Maya*. Cambridge University Press, New York, NY.

Kennett, Douglas J., Keith M. Prufer, Brendan J. Culleton, Richard J. George, Mark Robinson, Willa R. Trask, Gina M. Buckley, Emily Moes, Emily J. Kate, Thomas K. Harper, Lexi O'Donnell, Erin E. Ray, Ethan C. Hill, Asia Alsgaard, Christopher Merriman, Clayton Meredith, Heather J. H. Edgar, Jaime J. Awe, and Said M. Gutierrez. 2020. "Early Isotopic Evidence for Maize as a Staple Grain in the Americas." *Science Advances* 6(23): eaba3245.

McAnany, Patricia A. 2013. *Living with the Ancestors: Kinship and Kingship in Ancient Maya Society*. Revised ed. Cambridge University Press, Cambridge.

Martin, Simon. 2006. "Cacao in Ancient Maya Religion: First Fruit from the Maize Tree and other Tales from the Underworld." In *Chocolate in Mesoamerica: A Cultural History of Cacao*, Cameron McNeil (ed.), pp. 154–83. University Press of Florida, Gainesville, FL.

Martin, Simon. 2015. "The Old Man of the Maya Universe: Unified Aspects to Ancient Maya Religion." In *Maya Archaeology 3*, Stephen D. Houston, Charles W. Golden, and Joel Skidmore (eds), pp. 186–226. Precolumbia Mesoweb Press, San Francisco, CA.

Martin, Simon, and Nikolai Grube. 2008. *Chronicle of the Maya Kings and Queens: Deciphering the Dynasties of the Ancient Maya*. 2nd ed. Thames & Hudson, London.

Milbrath, Susan, and Carlos Peraza Lope. 2003. "Revisiting Mayapan: Mexico's Last Maya Capital." *Ancient Mesoamerica* 14(1): 1–46.

Monaghan, John D. 2000. "Theology and History in the Study of Mesoamerican Religions." In *Supplement to the Handbook of Middle American Indians, Vol. 6: Ethnology*, Victoria R. Bricker and John D. Monaghan (eds), pp. 24–49. University of Texas Press, Austin, TX.

Palka, Joel W. 2005. *Unconquered Lacandon Maya: Ethnohistory and Archaeology of Indigenous Culture Change*. University Press of Florida, Gainesville, FL.

Proskouriakoff, Tatiana. 1993. *Maya History*. University of Texas Press, Austin, TX.

Quilter, Jeffrey. 1990. "The Moche Revolt of the Objects." *Latin American Antiquity* 1(1): 42–65.

Restall, Matthew. 2004. "Maya Ethnogenesis." *Journal of Latin American Anthropology* 9(1): 64–89.

Restall, Matthew, and Florine Asselbergs (eds). 2007. *Invading Guatemala: Spanish, Nahua, and Maya Accounts of the Conquest Wars*. The Pennsylvania State University Press, University Park, PA.

Ringle, William M. 2020. "The Northern Maya Tollans." In *The Maya World*, Scott R. Hutson and Traci Ardren (eds), pp. 752–72. Routledge, Abingdon.

Sachse, Frauke. 2008. "Over Distant Waters: Places of Origin and Creation in Colonial K'iche'an Sources." In *Pre-Columbian Landscapes of Creation and Origin*, John E. Staller (ed.), pp. 123–60. Springer, New York, NY.

Salomon, Frank. 1999. "Testimonies: The Making and Reading of Native South American Historical Sources." In *The Cambridge History of the Native Peoples of the Americas. Volume 3, South America, Part 1*, Frank Salomon and Stuart B. Schwartz (eds), pp. 19–95. Cambridge University Press, Cambridge.

Schackt, Jon. 2001. "The Emerging Maya: A Case of Ethnogenesis." In *Maya Survivalism*, Ueli Hostettler and Matthew Restall (eds), pp. 3–14. Anton Saurwein, Markt Schwaben.

Scherer, Andrew K. 2015. *Mortuary Landscapes of the Classic Maya: Rituals of Body and Soul*. University of Texas Press, Austin, TX.

Sparks, Garry. 2019. *Rewriting Maya Religion: Domingo de Vico, K'iche' Maya Intellectuals, and the Theologia Indorum*. University Press of Colorado, Louisville, CO.

Stuart, David. 2004. "New Year Records in Classic Maya Inscriptions." *The PARI Journal* 5: 1–6.

Taladoire, Eric. 2001. "The Architectural Background of the Pre-Hispanic Ballgame-An Evolutionary Perspective." In *The Sport of Life and Death: The Mesoamerican Ballgame*, E. Michael Whittington (ed.), pp. 96–115. Thames & Hudson, London.

Taube, Karl A. 1985. "The Classic Maya Maize God: A Reappraisal." In *Fifth Palenque Round Table, 1983*, Virginia M. Fields (ed.), pp. 171–81. Pre-Columbian Art Research Institute, San Francisco.

Taube, Karl A. 2009. "The Maya Maize God and the Mythic Origins of Dance." In *The Maya and their Sacred Narratives: Text and Context in Maya Mythologies. Proceedings of the 12th European Maya Conference, Geneva, December 7–8, 2007*, Geneviève Le Fort, Raphaël Gardiol, Sebastian Matteo, and Christophe Helmke (eds), pp. 41–52. Anton Saurwein, Markt Schwaben.

Tiesler, Vera, and Guilhem Olivier. 2020. "Open Chests and Broken Hearts: Ritual Sequences and Meanings of Human Heart Sacrifice in Mesoamerica." *Current Anthropology* 61(2): 168–93.

Vail, Gabrielle. 2004. "A Reinterpretation of *Tzolk'in* Almanacs in the Madrid Codex." In *The Madrid Codex: New Approaches to Understanding an Ancient Maya Manuscript*, Gabrielle Vail and Anthony F. Aveni (eds), pp. 215–52. University Press of Colorado, Boulder, CO.

van Akkeren, Ruud W. 2003. "Authors of the Popol Wuj." *Ancient Mesoamerica* 14(2): 237–56.

Zender, Marc. 2014. "On the Reading of Three Classic Maya Portrait Glyphs." *The PARI Journal* 15: 1–14.

ACKNOWLEDGMENTS

Writing this book has been an adventure, and thankfully not a solo one. I am grateful to Ben Hayes and India Jackson, my ever-enthusiastic editorial guides; to Jen Moore for her careful copy-editing; and to the intrepid Sally Nicholls for securing the images that bring life to the pages. Many thanks to Stephen Houston and Simon Martin for setting me down this path and to Frauke Sachse, Michael Dürr, and Nils Jansen for accompanying me during early brainstorming. Sarah Newman and Franco Rossi provided a key lead for the armadillo image, and Simon Martin was especially generous in sharing his many drawings. I extend my profound gratitude to Artem Malykh, Monica Matsumoto, and especially Erika Milam and Dorothee Arndt for courageously volunteering to be the manuscript's first readers and for their generous feedback. I am indebted to the Wissenschaftskolleg zu Berlin, the Alexander von Humboldt Foundation, and Iken Paap at the Ibero-Amerikanisches Institut in Berlin, for giving me all the time, support, and community that I could have wanted for this journey.

SOURCES OF ILLUSTRATIONS

a = above; **b** = below; **l** = left; **r** = right

Photo Lucy Brown/Adobe Stock **125**; akg-images/De Agostini Picture Library/G. Dagli Orti **21**; Associated Press/Alamy Stock Photo **65**; Georgios Kollidas/Alamy Stock Photo **199**; John Mitchell/Alamy Stock Photo **63**; World History Archive/Alamy Stock Photo **95**, **135**; Courtesy of Bonampak Documentation Project, illustration by Heather Hurst and Leonard Ashby **196**; Museum of Fine Arts, Boston **145**; Museum of Fine Arts, Houston/ Gift of Frank Carroll in memory of Clytie Allen/Bridgeman Images **115**; after Carmack and Mondloch, *El Título de Totonicapán*, Mexico City, 1983 **162**; after Castillo, *Yaxha laguna Encantada: Naturaleza, arquelogía y conservacíon*, Guatemala City, 1999 **94**; Art Institute of Chicago **103**; Photo by Alfredo Gálvez Suárez, CIRMA **159**; © Sjors737/Dreamstime. com **139**; Sächische Landesbibliothek - Staats-und Universitätsbiliothek Dresden **37**, **42**, **50**, **123l**; Godman et al., *Biologia Centrali-Americana: Zoology, Botany and Archaeology*, London, 1879 **29**; Universidad Francisco Marroquin, Guatemala **193**; Heather Hurst, ©2004 **106**; Trustees of the British Museum, London **123r**; Bruce Love **160**; Museum of the Americas, Madrid **33**, **43**, **45a**, **55**, **69**, **97**, **181**; Courtesy Simon Martin **107**, **128**, **133**, **153**; Mallory Matsumoto **188**; © 2025 Maya Woman: The Helen Moran Collection. All rights reserved **81**, **109**, **140**, **148**, **171**; Courtesy Oswaldo Chinchilla Mazariegos **62**; The Metropolitan Museum of Art, New York **137**; Digital Image © 2012 Fray Angélico Chávez History Library, NMHM **156**, **202**; Courtesy of the Peabody Museum of Archaeology and Ethnology, Harvard University **166**, **173**, **176**; Gift of the Carnegie Institution of Washington, 1950. © President and Fellows of Harvard College, Peabody Museum of Archaeology and Ethnology, Harvard University **113**, **183**, **187**; Peabody Museum Expedition, E. H. Thompson, Director, 1907–1910. Courtesy of the Peabody Museum of Archaeology and Ethnology, Harvard University **75**; Courtesy of the Penn Museum, image 64-5-108 **16**; Jorge Perez de Lara **1**, **2**, **67**, **73**, **79**, **82**, **89**, **111**, **184**, **204**; Princeton University Art Museum **49**; Princeton University Library **31**, **34**, **39**, **200**; Drawing by Linda Schele © David Schele/Photo courtesy Ancient Americas at LACMA **117**, **126**, **155**; Gianni Dagli Orti/Shutterstock **105**; Donnebryant/Shutterstock **70**; photograph by Robert Słaboński (Proyecto Conservación de los Murales de Chajul) **194**; Drawing by David Stuart **60**; © Thames & Hudson Ltd. **121**; Archivio Fotografico Manuel Toussaint. IIE-UNAM **87**; From *Images from the Underground* by Andrea J. Stone, © 1995. By permission of the University of Texas Press **142**; Justin Kerr Maya Archive, Dumbarton Oaks, Trustees for Harvard University, Washington, D.C. **11**, **13**, **48**, **51**, **53**, **58**, **61**, **76**, **88**, **93**, **99**, **119**, **129**, **131**; Moche Archive, Dumbarton Oaks, Trustees for Harvard University, Washington, D.C. **45b**; Smithsonian American Art Museum, Washington, D.C. **143**, **164**; Drawing by Marc Zender **130**.

INDEX

Page numbers in *italics* refer to illustrations.